Thabo Mbeki

OHIO SHORT HISTORIES OF AFRICA

This series of Ohio Short Histories of Africa is meant for those who are looking for a brief but lively introduction to a wide range of topics in African history, politics, and biography, written by some of the leading experts in their fields.

Thabo Mbeki

Adekeye Adebajo

OHIO UNIVERSITY PRESS

ATHENS

Ohio University Press, Athens, Ohio 45701
www.ohioswallow.com

First published by Jacana Media (Pty) Ltd in 2014
10 Orange Street
Sunnyside
Auckland Park 2092
South Africa
+27 011 628 3200
www.jacana.co.za

First published in North America in 2017 by Ohio University Press
Printed in the United States of America
Ohio University Press books are printed on acid-free paper ⊚ ™

ISBN: 978-0-8214-2274-8
e-ISBN: 978-0-8214-4605-8

Library of Congress Cataloging-in-Publication Data available

Contents

Introduction

Thabo Mbeki is the most important African political figure of his generation. From June 1999 until September 2008 he was leader of Africa's most industrialised state, having succeeded the revered Nelson Mandela as president of post-apartheid South Africa. Even before then, Mbeki ran the country as *de facto* prime minister under President Mandela, who for the most part handed over the reins of power to his heir apparent shortly after assuming the presidency in May 1994. As a key leader of the African National Congress (ANC) in exile, Mbeki had, from the 1960s, played a significant role in the anti-apartheid struggle, under the mentorship of the ANC president Oliver Tambo, and then led secret talks to end apartheid with the white South African corporate sector, Afrikaner intellectuals and National Party officials in the late 1980s. Between 1990 and 1994, during the negotiations for a political settlement, Mbeki played an important part in laying the foundations for a post-apartheid state and establishing what would become one of the most respected constitutional democracies in the world. He had thus dedicated 52 years of his life to the ANC and to the politics of his country by the time of his sudden ousting from power by his own party in September 2008.

As a historical figure, it is important to place Mbeki within an African context. As this book explains, his sense of belonging to the wider African continent and his later vision of an African Renaissance were inspired by his upbringing, education and career in exile. He was critically shaped by the two decades he spent in exile in Swaziland, Botswana, Nigeria and Zambia between 1971 and 1990. His time in Nigeria as head of the ANC office there, between December 1976 and early 1978, was particularly significant. Not only did Africa's largest country provide him with an example of black self-assertion and cultural authenticity, but he also forged an enduring relationship with the military head of state, Olusegun Obasanjo (1976–9), which would later enable him to promote peacemaking in Africa and build pan-African institutions like the African Union (AU), the New Partnership for Africa's Development (NEPAD), and the African Peer Review Mechanism (APRM) when both men were in power as elected heads of state between 1999 and 2007.

In understanding the importance of Mbeki as a

political figure, I have sought to compare him with Ghana's legendary first president, Kwame Nkrumah, who was in power between 1957 and 1966. Both were philosopher-kings who articulated bold pan-African visions and generated ideas to which other leaders were forced to respond. Both were, however, political prophets whose compelling visions were ultimately unfulfilled. Both also ruled in a monarchical fashion, imperiously dominating decision-making within their respective parties, though Mbeki – unlike Nkrumah – adhered strictly to constitutional rules. Both men are likely to be remembered more for their pan-African achievements in foreign policy than for their domestic policies.

Mbeki was a complex figure, full of contradictions and paradoxes: a rural child who became an urban sophisticate; a prophet of Africa's Renaissance who was also an anglophile; a committed young Marxist who, while in power, embraced conservative economic policies and protected white corporate interests; a rational and dispassionate thinker who was particularly sensitive to criticism and dissent; a champion of African self-reliance who relied excessively on foreign capital and promoted a continental economic plan – NEPAD – that was disproportionately dependent on foreign aid; and a thoughtful intellectual who supported policies on HIV/AIDS that withheld antiretroviral drugs from infected people, resulting in hundreds of thousands of preventable deaths.

Some may object to the approach of the 'Great Man' view of history pioneered by Thomas Carlyle, in his famous book *On Heroes, Hero-Worship, and the Heroic in History* (1841). Carlyle argued that history can be analysed through the actions, ideas, charisma and political skills of great historical figures. My own study does not wish to deny that our subject has been shaped by his social environment and that other individuals and institutions – the ANC, its alliance partners, the business sector, civil society, and African and external actors – played more than an instrumental role in the events described here. A biography of Mbeki, though, helps us to understand events through the actions and ideas of a powerful individual who was the dominant figure in South African politics for 14 years. Mbeki's was an 'imperial presidency', and his monarchical style of rule saw him dominate decision-making within his party and government. It is thus legitimate to focus attention on his actions and ideas in interacting with other key players to explain the epoch in which he held power. The book also touches on Mbeki's relationship with six key figures who helped shape his political beliefs and achievements: his father Govan Mbeki, Oliver Tambo, Joe Slovo, Chris Hani, Nelson Mandela and Olusegun Obasanjo.

I lived in South Africa through the last five years of Mbeki's presidency, and thus witnessed at first hand the optimism unleashed by his vision of an African Renaissance as well as the tragic downfall of a flawed but intellectually brilliant leader. It seems foolhardy to attempt – even in a short biography – an assessment of the most important African political figure of his generation. Three key reasons have motivated me to embark on this brief intellectual journey. First, I felt a need to place Mbeki in a pan-African as much as a South African context. This book highlights his intellectual and lived experiences that shaped his pan-Africanism and African Renaissance vision, as well as the perspectives of diverse African scholars. Second, the crucial point that Mbeki's biographies – even the finest and most definitive one by Mark Gevisser[1] – have hitherto missed is that his legacy lies in the area of foreign policy: mainly his peacemaking efforts in the Democratic Republic of the Congo (DRC), Burundi, Zimbabwe and Côte d'Ivoire, as well as his initiatives to build African institutions to promote regional integration, democratic governance, and peace. These policies were not always successful, but they were often pursued with vigour and vision. Finally, I was inspired, as a Nigerian author living in South Africa, not only to present a pan-African analysis, but to try to help correct the glaring absence of black authors as biographers of African political figures.

1

Africa's philosopher-kings

The idea of the philosopher-king is derived from Plato's *Republic*, in which, as part of a vision of the just city, the best form of government is said to be one in which philosophers rule.[1] The philosopher is the only person who can rule well, since they are intellectually and morally suited for this role, and they are expected to employ their knowledge of goodness and virtue to assist their citizens to achieve these ends. Plato's mentor, Socrates, famously remarked: 'Until philosophers rule as kings in their cities, or those who are nowadays called kings and leading men become genuine and adequate philosophers … cities will have no rest from evils.'[2] For Socrates, the philosopher was a lover of wisdom and a seer committed to a perennial quest for the truth.

The biblical saying that prophets are not honoured in their own land epitomises the fate of two African philosopher-kings: South Africa's second post-apartheid president, Thabo Mbeki (1999–2008) and Ghana's founding president, Kwame Nkrumah (1957–1966). Despite perverse attempts to compare him with men like South African prime minister Jan Smuts,[3] Mbeki's political leadership must in fact be understood within an African context. Mbeki can in some ways be regarded as the present age's Nkrumah. Both Mbeki and Nkrumah believed in Africa's ancient glory and sought to build modern states that restored the continent's past. Both were Renaissance men: visionary and cosmopolitan intellectuals committed to pan-Africanism and to restoring the dignity of black people whether in Harare, Harlem or Haiti.

Both Nkrumah and Mbeki were instrumental in the creation of pan-African organisations: in Nkrumah's case the Organisation of African Unity (OAU) and in Mbeki's the African Union (AU). While Nkrumah championed the African Personality, Mbeki promoted the African Renaissance, both widely used but nebulous concepts that lacked clear definition or a road-map of how to operationalise them in practice. Both leaders were also peacemakers. Nkrumah sent troops to the Congo in 1960 to assist a United Nations peacekeeping mission and was himself on a peace mission to Vietnam when his government was toppled in a coup d'état in February 1966. For his part, Mbeki strove to make peace in the Democratic Republic of the Congo, Burundi and Côte d'Ivoire, and sent peacekeeping troops to the Congo, Burundi and Sudan's Darfur region. Both leaders sought to speak on behalf of Africa in multilateral forums, often to the irritation of other regional leaders. Both were accused of monarchical tendencies, and both in the end were toppled in apparent acts of regicide: Nkrumah by the military, and Mbeki by his own party.

But there were clear differences between the two. Nkrumah was charismatic and, for a while, enjoyed the unparalleled adulation of the Ghanaian people. Mbeki did not inherit the charisma of his predecessor as president, the Nobel Peace laureate Nelson Mandela, and relied on other means, notably a form of technocracy, to rule. Nkrumah was able to mobilise and rally the masses; Mbeki relied on political manoeuvring within the ANC to maintain and exercise power. Nkrumah favoured a more federalist United States of Africa; Mbeki's vision of regional integration was more gradualist. Nkrumah adopted a personality cult and 'Nkrumahism' was developed into an anti-imperial ideology of pan-Africanism; Mbeki avoided a personality cult and no ideology bearing the name 'Mbeki-ism' ever came into existence during his rule.

Mbeki's ANC and Nkrumah's Convention People's Party (CPP) were electorally dominant, and both leaders used their parties as elite-driven vanguard organisations, ruling in a top-down fashion and seeing themselves as guardians of the 'national revolution'. Nkrumah deployed CPP cadres in a bid to transform the colonial civil service; while Mbeki deployed ANC cadres in an attempt to transform the apartheid bureaucracy. Both were masters of political intrigue and manipulation. Both could be indecisive in making difficult decisions, and often left unpleasant tasks to lieutenants, avoiding direct confrontation. Both stressed party discipline and personal loyalty. Both allowed a climate of fear to reign within their parties. The ANC and the CPP came not only to be closely identified with the state, but also fell under the control of their powerful leaders. Their closest supporters, lacking an independent power base, became dependent on their masters, and tended towards sycophancy and subservience. Both leaders doled out patronage through state agencies and managed their parliamentary parties with an iron grip. Both railed against corruption, and were widely perceived as being personally more interested in power than wealth (though seeming to condone some instances of corruption, especially in favour of their parties, while failing to rein in wayward lieutenants). Both also sought to prevent the ascendancy of an organised 'left'.

In power, Nkrumah and Mbeki became increasingly sensitive to suspected plots and conspiracies, with Nkrumah deeply affected by two assassination attempts. Both were nocturnal workaholics who survived on only a few hours' sleep, with Mbeki famously surfing the internet late at night. Both were pragmatic politicians who dispensed with ideology if they felt that it impeded the achievement of practical goals. Both regarded themselves as philosopher-kings who sought the company of fellow intellectuals, though many members of the intelligentsia were opposed to their rule. Both indulged literary tastes: Nkrumah had 14 publications to his name, while Mbeki published three books of speeches, many of which he wrote himself. Both seemed to focus disproportionately on foreign policy as they tired of incessant party squabbles. Both tried to run foreign policy from well-staffed presidential units, and both are likely to be remembered in the long term more for their foreign policies than for their domestic achievements.

Despite some histrionic depictions of Mbeki as a dictator, it was Nkrumah's rule that in fact represented real autocracy: the Ghanaian leader outlawed the opposition, established one-party rule, smashed civil society, banned most labour action, censored the media, and bullied the judiciary. Another aspect of Nkrumah's rule that Mbeki never replicated was a personality cult. In this regard, perhaps Zimbabwe's Robert Mugabe may provide a closer contemporary comparison for Nkrumah's autocratic rule, and Libya's Muammar Qaddafi for his pan-African federalism.

It is also important when placing Mbeki in an African context of monarchical and prophetic rule to note some of the influences – conscious or unconscious – on his political leadership style derived from his two decades in African exile. Between 1971 and 1990 Mbeki lived in

Botswana, Swaziland, Nigeria and Zambia. Two of the African leaders with whom Mbeki worked closest during these years – Zambia's Kenneth Kaunda and Tanzania's Julius Nyerere – were themselves philosopher-kings and political prophets who attempted to provide visionary leadership in their own countries. Their leadership styles would influence Mbeki when he came to power as president of South Africa, though he stuck closely in his own presidency to constitutional rules, never moving towards the one-party autocracy of some of his fellow African leaders.

In placing Mbeki in a historical African context, it is important to assess briefly a few concepts and typologies of leadership style in Africa, in particular the monarchical and prophetic traditions in African politics. I do not wish to present an exaggerated picture of the influence of individual leaders (even powerful ones) in shaping events solely through their own actions, nor do I wish to ignore the fact that other actors, institutions and variables had an effect on events that occurred during their rule. The main purpose of my approach is to contextualise the leadership style, performance and legacy of some important African political leaders of their generation.

The Kenyan scholar Ali Mazrui was one of the early pioneers in the study of personal rule and leadership styles in Africa. He remarked that African leaders have attempted to use monarchical forms 'to strengthen the legitimacy of the regimes with sacred symbols and romantic awe'.[4]

Mazrui further saw monarchical tendencies in African political culture as part of the need of many African leaders to revive a splendid past in order to restore a sense of national dignity that had been damaged by the effects of centuries of slavery and European imperialism. In respect of Kwame Nkrumah, Mazrui noted that the Ghanaian president exhibited a certain flamboyance derived from a sense of racial humiliation and awe of British royalty, which was expressed in terms of a monarchical tendency in his own leadership style. Nkrumah had lived in Britain for two years during his exile. He admired British institutions, was proud of being the first African to be appointed by Queen Elizabeth to her Privy Council, and, when president, employed a British chief of army staff, a British attorney-general, and a British private secretary. As leader, Nkrumah sought simultaneously to ancientise and modernise his country, taking the name of the ancient African empire of Ghana while embarking on an industrialisation project in a bid to replicate the economic success of Western societies.

Like Nkrumah, Thabo Mbeki similarly sought to modernise South Africa and to restore Africa's past glory through his promotion of an African Renaissance. When in office he concentrated power and decision-making in the Presidency and wielded close control of his party and of parliament, appointing all the provincial premiers as well as the most senior members of the civil service. Although Mbeki may not have used sacred symbols to strengthen his rule, he certainly made use of the power

19

of what Mazrui calls 'romantic awe'. His references to and invocation of the prose of pan-Africanists like W.E.B. Du Bois, Kwame Nkrumah and Walter Rodney as well as the poetry of Aimé Césaire, Langston Hughes and Léopold Senghor served to legitimise his role as the president of the last African country to be liberated from alien rule.

In his most famous essay, written in 1966 shortly after Nkrumah fell from power, Mazrui depicted the Ghanaian leader as a 'Leninist Czar', a royalist revolutionary.[5] The Kenyan scholar argued that Nkrumah had ruled in a monarchical fashion and thus forfeited the organisational effectiveness of a Leninist party structure. The Ghanaian leader had wanted 'Nkrumahism' to leave a similar historical and revolutionary mark to that of Leninism. As Mazrui noted, 'Nkrumah's tragedy was a tragedy of *excess*, rather than of contradiction. He tried to be too much of a revolutionary monarch.' Mazrui concluded that Nkrumah would be celebrated more as a great pan-African than as a great Ghanaian, an insight that has proved to be accurate.

The second typology of African leadership that is helpful in understanding Mbeki is that of the prophetic ruler. As Robert Jackson and Carl Rosberg, in their innovative study *Personal Rule in Black Africa*, noted: 'The prophet, political or religious, is a revolutionary – that is, one who prophesies a better future, whose attainment requires the radical transformation of the present.'[6] Two key characteristics are associated with prophetic rulers.

Firstly, these leaders are charismatic: they have charm

and mystique, and their personality is often closely tied to their prophetic rule. This charisma draws people to them, and in turn they feed their followers with their oratorical brilliance and magnetic presence. Prophets express the hopes, resentments and fears of their people, and they are the living embodiment of popular aspirations for a better future.

African prophetic leaders like Nkrumah have set out to develop personality cults in which they are deified and worshipped unquestioningly. Like European monarchs of old, prophetic rulers in Africa have sought to embody the state: it is in them that sovereignty resides. The royal European expression *L'état, c'est moi* (I am the state) has found resonance in contemporary Africa. Though lacking the charisma and mobilising skills of Nkrumah, Mbeki showed signs of prophetic rule in his lyrical oratory and vision of an African Renaissance which prophesied that Africa would own the twenty-first century. He thus sought, as a prophetic leader, to chart a glorious future for the continent's socio-economic renewal.

The second main feature of prophetic rule is its religious dimension. This rule often becomes singleminded in achieving its goals, as sacrifice and the suspension of immediate political and economic desires are urged on followers in order to bring about the 'revolution'. As in the religious sphere, the rewards of the people await them in heaven, and they are therefore urged to forgo the possession of 'earthly' material things until the paradise arrives, though it must be said that African political prophets have sometimes built their own mansions on earth. At the present stage of Africa's socio-economic development, miracles have proved difficult to perform, as the stuff of which miracles are made has been in short supply. Economic development is, after all, a painstaking, gradual process which requires decades of careful planning, adequate capital and competent technocrats to achieve. The vision of paradise which overwhelmed religious disciples and guaranteed their adherence to the true faith is simply not within the African prophet's capacity to bring about rapidly, as the cases of Nkrumah and Mbeki proved. It is this failure to fortify the faith of the people through healing and other signs of divine approbation – rapid socio-economic development, the elimination of poverty, and the transformation of society – that cost both Nkrumah and Mbeki their political lives.

Finally, Nkrumah and Mbeki can also be seen as tragic figures in African Shakespearian dramas. Whereas Nkrumah might be viewed as a Julius Caesar, Coriolanus best mirrors Mbeki's fate. Nkrumah's biographer Bankole Timothy observes that the Ghanaian leader was accused of trying to build 'a great African Empire with himself as Caesar'.[7] As Shakespeare's play recounts, the Roman Senate made Caesar perpetual dictator of Rome, just as the Ghanaian parliament effectively made Nkrumah Ghana's dictator. Both Caesar and Nkrumah fell from power after suspicions arose that they would turn their republics into monarchies, and both were betrayed by close associates and lieutenants. Four decades after the military had toppled Nkrumah in a coup, Mbeki paid a melancholy tribute to Nkrumah's tragic fate when he reflected: 'We were mere schoolboys when we saw the black star rise on our firmament, as the colonial Gold Coast crowned itself with the ancient African name of Ghana. We knew then that the promise we had inherited would be honoured. The African giant was awakening! But it came to pass that the march of African time snatched away that promise. Very little seemed to remain along its path except the footprints of despair.'[8]

As Mbeki's finest biographer, Mark Gevisser, reminds us, during his student days in Moscow Mbeki's favourite play had been Shakespeare's *Coriolanus*. This was the tragedy of a heroic Roman soldier whose demise was brought about by his obduracy and pride. Like *Julius Caesar*, it is a play about politics and betrayal. Coriolanus becomes a war hero, is banished from Rome, defects to the Volscians, and is subsequently killed. But rather than the conventional perception of Coriolanus as a 'vainglorious proto-fascist' and a 'tyrant driven by hubris', Mbeki instead regarded the Roman soldier as the model for a twentieth-century revolutionary, noting that Coriolanus was full of 'truthfulness, courage, self-sacrifice, absence of self-seeking, brotherliness, heroism, optimism'. Mbeki admired Coriolanus for being prepared to go to war against his own people, whom he described

23

as 'rabble … an unthinking mob, with its cowardice, its lying, its ordinary people-ness'.[9] The similarity of the fates of Coriolanus and Mbeki is eerie: both were seen as aloof and arrogant; both refused to kowtow to popular perceptions of how a leader should behave; and both were ultimately brought down by character flaws of obduracy and arrogance.

2

Coming of age

Thabo Mvuyelwa Mbeki was born in the village of Mbewuleni near Idutywa in the rural Transkei (now the Eastern Cape province) on 18 June 1942.[1] The area – whose landscape is marked by mountains, hills, rivers, hamlets and homesteads – is the home of Xhosa speakers, who were among the earliest indigenous South Africans to convert in large numbers to Christianity, acquire a missionary education and participate in the colonial economy. From this educated, acculturated class came the future leaders of the African nationalist movement in South Africa. Indeed, the Eastern Cape has provided much of the ANC's leadership from its inception in 1912. (Nelson Mandela was also a member of what is sometimes referred to as the 'Xhosa Nostra'.)

Thabo was the eldest son of Govan and Epainette Mbeki. His parents were middle-class *izifundiswa* (educated ones) and communists, whose own fathers had been peasant farmers and devout Christians, part of the Westernised elite. Both Govan and Epainette were deeply involved in the struggle for racial justice in South Africa until their deaths in 2001 and 2014 respectively.

Thabo's father, Govan – affectionately referred to by younger peers as 'Oom Gov' – was a teacher and journalist, who attended the same Methodist missionary secondary school as Mandela – Healdtown in Fort Beaufort – where he excelled in Latin. He went on to study politics and psychology at Fort Hare University College, whose famous alumni would include such future ANC leaders as Mandela and Oliver Tambo. This elite black university in the Eastern Cape trained as well many of the first generation of post-independence African leaders such as Zimbabwe's Robert Mugabe and Joshua Nkomo, and Botswana's Seretse Khama.

While at Fort Hare, Govan was influenced ideologically by two young white communists – Eddie and Win Roux – who were on a proselytising honeymoon in the Eastern Cape. He became a lifelong communist and would later name his eldest son after his close friend and ideological mentor, Edwin Thabo Mofutsanyana, one of the leading lights in the Communist Party of South Africa. Epainette and Govan met at a secondary school in Durban where both were then teaching and were married in 1940. They then moved to Mbewuleni, where they set up one of the first black-owned general dealer's stores – and village post office – in rural Transkei to serve the *amaqaba*: the traditionally minded, largely illiterate peasants of the village. Govan would later sell insurance and become involved in work for the ANC, while Epainette looked after the shop and the family's four children: Linda (born 1941), Thabo (1942), Moeletsi (1945) and Jama (1948).

Thabo's mother, Epainette, was, like her husband, a teacher who had graduated from a famous missionary training college and school, Adams College, in Natal. Under the influence of Betty du Toit, an Afrikaner communist, she became only the second black female member of the Communist Party. Epainette is said to have had a greater role in shaping the political views of Thabo and his siblings than their strict father.

Even before he was convicted at the Rivonia Trial in 1964 and sentenced to jail for life, Govan's marriage to Epainette appears to have broken down amid financial difficulties. He had by then long lived apart from his wife and children, having left home to take up a teaching job in Ladysmith in Natal, from which he was fired for his political activism. Govan then moved in 1953 to Port Elizabeth, where he worked for the ANC and edited the left-wing newspaper *New Age* (later renamed *Spark*), which were both banned by the apartheid government.

Govan was an ideologically doctrinaire man who held strongly, even stubbornly, to his views and opinions: characteristics that his eldest son, Thabo, would also display. Because of Govan's absence, Thabo grew up largely without his father, and Govan's relationship with his son was always somewhat distant. At home the family patriarch buried himself in his reading and busied himself with his activism, leaving the children largely to the care of their mother. As he later admitted: 'I never really had time for the children … Probably they felt that I didn't pay sufficient attention to them … I wouldn't blame them if they felt like that.'[2] It is hard to tell exactly what impact this lack of paternal affection had on Thabo, but it seems to have contributed to his introverted and sensitive nature. When asked about the disappearance of his youngest son, Jama, and Thabo's own son, Kwanda, in exile, Govan unsentimentally remarked: 'When you go into war, if your comrade in front of you falls on his horse, you must not stop and weep. You jump over him into battle. You learn not to weep.'[3]

* * *

Thabo certainly inherited his father's sense of dress and his eloquence and articulateness, but also his coldness and emotional reserve as well as his singleminded focus on the liberation struggle. At the first meeting between father and son in Lusaka, Zambia, in January 1990 after nearly three decades of not having seen each other, Govan greeted Thabo by formally shaking hands with him, as he did with other comrades lined up to meet the recently released Rivonia trialists, while other families like the Sisulus broke ranks and exchanged warm and joyous embraces. As Govan noted to a reporter at the time: 'You must remember that Thabo Mbeki is no longer my son. He is my comrade.'[4] But both Govan and Thabo did later share moments of private affection.

Thabo was greatly inspired by his father's example to succeed, and seemed determined to prove himself to Govan by excelling intellectually and politically and carrying on the family's tradition of *noblesse oblige*. As Thabo remarked in exile, 'what I'm doing here, I want to do in the best way I can. I want to excel at it and complete the work of my father.'[5] The son was also keen to escape his father's shadow and succeed on his own terms rather than as the scion of a famous struggle family. In the absence of his own father, the ANC would become Thabo's family for 52 years, and the ANC president Oliver Tambo, with whom Thabo worked closely for 30 years, would become an adopted father and political mentor.

Like Govan, the young Thabo was – and remains – a voracious reader, consuming the books in the family home: English poetry, Marxist literature (including the *Communist Manifesto*), James Aggrey, Dostoyevsky, A.C. Jordan's famous Xhosa novel *Ingqumbo yemiNyanya* (The Wrath of the Ancestors) and even his father's own volume of critical essays, *Transkei in the Making* (1939). Govan and Epainette adopted a Socratic method in educating their children, and did not try to indoctrinate them. As Thabo later noted, 'Our parents never initiated any political discussions at home. It was always up to us to raise matters

29

with them, then they would talk about it.'[6] From an early age Govan's eldest son wrote and read letters for illiterate villagers in his community to and from their migrant family members working on the mines and in domestic service across South Africa. Along with his siblings, they were exposed at an early age to the poverty of South Africa's black majority and the awful conditions of black mineworkers who came back to the village to die of lung disease. As a young boy Thabo attended the local primary school. Though a good student, he did not like maths and played truant to avoid classes until Epainette discovered the problem, and gave him private lessons at home.

From the age of eight, Thabo was sent away to live with various relatives across the country, as both Govan and Epainette believed it was best that their children should live apart from their politically active parents, who constantly faced the threat of arrest. This nomadic existence created a sense of dislocation even before Thabo left South Africa to go into political exile. Practically orphaned and without a stable family and friends, he became somewhat of an introverted loner. Thabo attended a Moravian school in Queenstown, before going to the famous Scottish Presbyterian missionary secondary school of Lovedale College – the 'Eton of Africa' – in 1955. Lovedale was located in Alice on the banks of the Tyhume River in the Eastern Cape. Here, at an institution modelled on British public schools, where the pupils wore blazers, Mbeki became acquainted with the works of Shakespeare, Jane Austen and Joseph Conrad, as well as the Xhosa poetry of S.E.K. Mqhayi, the great 'poet of the nation'. For more than a century, black students from across southern Africa and latterly from further north, as far as Uganda, had attended the school and been prepared for leadership roles in their own communities and countries. Thabo was thus simultaneously exposed at Lovedale to a pan-African identity and to British traditions, both of which he would later come to embody.

Thabo entered Lovedale soon after the National Party (NP) came to power in 1948 and started implementing the racist policies of apartheid. In reaction, most students at Lovedale developed a heightened political consciousness. The year he entered, 1955, was the one in which the apartheid government ordered the forced removal of black residents from Sophiatown in Johannesburg. While at Lovedale Mbeki joined the ANC Youth League at the age of 14, learning to sing struggle songs in honour of the ANC president, Albert Luthuli, and the Congolese liberation hero, Patrice Lumumba. With students paid by the security police to spy on each other, the roots of Thabo's later suspicious nature and obsessive secrecy can perhaps be traced to his early political activism. His education at Lovedale was cut short after his involvement in a student strike – against poor food and the spying on, and expulsion of, students – in 1959. Thabo was expelled from the school and forced to return to his home at Mbewuleni. He took his matriculation exams in Umtata

31

that October, and obtained a disappointing second-class pass, a setback that strengthened his determination in future to achieve academic excellence.

* * *

At the age of 17, Mbeki became father to a son, Kwanda, born out of wedlock with Olive Nokwanda Mpahlwa. Thabo was thereafter banished from the Mpahlwa home, and denied access to his son. The boy was later reclaimed by Epainette, who looked after him and sent him away to boarding school. Kwanda was denied the paternal love that Thabo himself had missed while growing up. He later disappeared in 1981 under mysterious circumstances in an apparent elusive quest to join his father in Swaziland, and was never seen again.

Mbeki left the Eastern Cape for the first time at 17, arriving in Johannesburg in 1960, the *annus mirabilis* of independence for many African countries, but also the *annus horribilis* of the banning of the ANC and the Sharpeville massacre of 69 black protesters against the pass laws. Even at this young age, the precocious Thabo was regarded as clever and confident beyond his years. He became active in political organising for the underground ANC, and met two Indian South African brothers – Essop and Aziz Pahad – who would become lifelong friends and members of his cabinet (Essop also joined him at Sussex University in 1965). While in Johannesburg, Thabo lived for two years with the urbane ANC secretary-general, Duma Nokwe – the only black advocate at the Johannesburg bar – who became his first political mentor. Nokwe was seen by his critics as something of an elitist, far removed from the masses whose cause he claimed to be championing: a charge that would later be made about Mbeki too.

It was in Johannesburg that Thabo met Nelson Mandela for the first time in 1961, when the older man invited him for lunch at his Orlando West home. He also became acquainted with the ANC stalwart Walter Sisulu, who had been secretary-general before Nokwe. Mbeki was chosen as the first national secretary of the African Students' Association, which was a front for the recruitment of young members to the ANC. During this period he began to wear a pin of Vladimir Lenin on his lapel, as his communist intellectual awakening took shape. At the age of 20 Mbeki joined the underground South African Communist Party. He became involved in party cells and study groups, and was tutored by such communist leaders as Bram Fischer (who would defend Govan Mbeki, Nelson Mandela and others at the Rivonia Trial), J.B. Marks and Michael Harmel, from whom he absorbed Leninist ideas of a vanguard party. According to Lenin, the true revolutionary vanguardist forsakes both his family and class in order to join the masses he is called to lead: but though Thabo forsook his family, he certainly did not abandon his class.

Mbeki's first political writing appeared in the ANC-aligned newspaper *New Age* at this time, explaining why the association of African students had been formed and describing himself as part of 'the intellectual elite of a people [suffering] from subjection by a minority government'.[7] He also spent time travelling through South Africa and recruiting students on behalf of the ANC for training in Soviet universities. Thabo attended Britzius College in Johannesburg, passing – with the help of a friend and benefactor, Ann Welsh – his A-level exams in 1961 in economics, British economic history and British constitutional law, before completing a University of London junior degree in economics between 1961 and 1962. After the banning of the ANC in 1960, many of its leading members had gone into exile or had joined the underground military wing, Umkhonto we Sizwe (MK). Thabo was at first reluctant to leave the country, until Govan, then one of MK's High Command, intervened to tell him that he would be disowned by his family if he refused to go and was arrested while trying to wage 'armed struggle'. Govan would later imply that he did not feel his son was cut out to be a soldier.

On his way into exile with a group of students in September 1962, Thabo was arrested and jailed with his colleagues after crossing into white-ruled Rhodesia (now Zimbabwe). They were sent back to Bechuanaland (Botswana), before being transported with the help of the ANC to the Tanzanian capital of Dar es Salaam. This was where, in November 1962, Thabo first met the future

ANC president, Oliver Tambo, who had gone into exile in 1960. Tambo would become Mbeki's most important political mentor. Thabo was tasked by the then deputy president with leading a group of ANC students into exile, and Tambo arranged for him to fly with Kenneth Kaunda to London. The future Zambian president was travelling to the imperial capital to negotiate his country's independence. Also at the airport was the Tanzanian leader, Julius Nyerere.[8] This early exposure to these two African philosopher-kings would help shape Mbeki's pan-African commitment.

* * *

In 1962 Mbeki won admission on a scholarship to study economics – rather than the medicine his father had wanted him to pursue – at Sussex University in England, which had opened its doors only the year before. Thabo felt that he deserved to go to Oxford or Cambridge University,[9] but had to forgo the 'dreaming spires' of Oxbridge for the brick and concrete of Sussex. The new university's activism suited the young, doctrinaire disciple of Marxist-Leninist thinking. As a student, Thabo was tasked by the ANC with visiting Moscow on missions to meet ANC-supported South African students there. Though one of only a few black students at Sussex at the time (another, Peter Kenyatta, was the son of the Kenyan president), Thabo was elected to the university's Students' Union within three months of his arrival. He skilfully used this forum to mobilise town and gown in the seaside resort of Brighton to support the anti-apartheid struggle. While still a student, Mbeki led anti-apartheid political demonstrations across Britain, and testified to a session of the United Nations Special Committee against Apartheid, held in London in 1964, pleading for the South African government to spare the life of his father and those of his fellow Rivonia trialists. Thabo was also active in the international student movement, attending conferences in Algiers, Oslo, Moscow, Khartoum, Sofia and Ulan Bator.

At Sussex, Mbeki imbibed the ideas of Aimé Césaire, Léopold Senghor, W.E.B. Du Bois and Frantz Fanon. He also greatly admired the African-American civil rights leader Martin Luther King Jr. His master's thesis focused on industrialisation in West Africa (in particular, on small enterprises in Ghana and Nigeria), and his studies helped develop a pan-African awareness alongside a deepening of interest in the Western intellectual canon. It was at Sussex that Mbeki further engaged his passion for Shakespeare and W.B. Yeats, discovered the German playwright Bertolt Brecht, and began a lifelong interest in the African-American poets of the Harlem Renaissance of the 1920s, led by Langston Hughes. In a less intellectual expression of his pan-Africanism, Mbeki organised a party in Brighton for the West Indies cricket team, led by the legendary Garfield Sobers, in 1966.

It was also in England that Mbeki developed his urbane, cosmopolitan demeanour among a diverse group of friends. In exile later in Africa, he would complain to companions about being 'homesick' for England and longing for a 'pint of bitter'. Lacking a cultural core, the nomadic Mbeki necessarily improvised a polyglot identity that was neither completely African nor European, but instead borrowed from both worlds. In his later career, this prophet of the African Renaissance would often paradoxically cut the figure of a 'black Englishman', with his stiff and formal manner, English dress of sports jacket, designer suit or tweed cloth cap, and his fondness for Bay Rum tobacco as well as Scotch whisky. During his years in England, Mbeki was greatly influenced by British institutions and political culture. Walter Bagehot, the nineteenth-century essayist, had noted that the British political system – lacking a written constitution – represented a form of 'muddling through' and improvisation. It was a conservative system that preferred evolutionary to revolutionary change. Once in power as president of South Africa, Thabo's style came to resemble this political pragmatism, as did his peacemaking efforts across Africa.

Though he was strongly averse to direct confrontation, Thabo acquired a reputation, among some ANC colleagues, for being arrogant and ambitious. The fact that he had been sent by the ANC to England rather than the Soviet bloc, where most young ANC cadres studied, created particular resentment. A group of ANC students in Moscow, for example, refused to meet him in April 1967, dismissing him as a stooge of the party's leadership. That Mbeki stayed at the Tambo family home in north London during vacations from Sussex University further reinforced perceptions of special treatment, as the Tambos effectively adopted him as their own son. Though as a student he continued to fantasise about abandoning his studies to return home to join Umkhonto we Sizwe (MK), in the end he lobbied strongly to stay on at Sussex to do his master's in the Economics and Development programme between 1965 and 1966. Two economists at Sussex acted as important academic mentors in England: the Hungarian-born Tibor Barna, and the South African émigré Guy Routh. (Thabo's alma mater later awarded him an honorary doctorate in 1995.)

In both Johannesburg and Brighton, Mbeki had intimate relationships with white women. While at Sussex, he moved in with a younger student, Philippa Ingram, a step that South Africa's Immorality Act of 1950 would have prevented him from taking back home. In Johannesburg he had been romantically involved with the arts student and political activist Ann Nicholson, but the relationship had of necessity been more discreet. Nicholson's understanding of Mbeki and especially his leadership style is particularly insightful. She saw him as a conservative person who always took the path of least resistance, and did not want to rock the boat. She further noted that he had a deep sense of duty, believing that leaders could not have a personal life, but belonged to the movement.[10] This idea of the 'servant leader' embodied very much the same sense of selfless devotion often conveyed by the older generation of ANC leaders like his father Govan Mbeki, Nelson Mandela, Walter Sisulu and Oliver Tambo, from whom Thabo had directly or indirectly learned the art of politics. Thabo later remarked about the lessons he had imbibed from his foremost political mentor, Oliver Tambo: 'He taught me the obligation to understand the tasks of leadership, including the necessity never to tell lies, never to make false and unrealisable promises, never to say anything you do not mean or believe, and never to say anything that might evoke an enthusiastic populist response, but which would ultimately serve to undermine the credibility of our movement and struggle.'[11]

It was all of these formative experiences that helped to shape the future politics of Thabo Mbeki.

The path to power

After completing his education at Sussex University in
1966, Thabo Mbeki would devote his life fully to the anti-
apartheid struggle. His total dedication and commitment
were qualities that even his worst enemies had to concede.
From 1967 to 1969 he worked in the propaganda section
of the ANC office in London – its European headquarters
– where he came under the influence of senior leaders
like Yusuf Dadoo. His work focused largely on issues
such as nuclear disarmament; increases in fees for foreign
university students in Britain; and solidarity struggles
with the peoples of Zimbabwe, Angola, Mozambique and
Vietnam. Mbeki also campaigned for the re-election of
pipe-smoking Labour leader, Harold Wilson, in March
1966. His brother Moeletsi had arrived in London a year
earlier, and complained to Adelaide Tambo that Thabo
paid more attention to other comrades and did not talk

much to him. Similar to the way his father had acted towards him, Thabo explained to the ANC matriarch that he did not intend to give his younger brother any special treatment over other comrades.[1]

During this period, Thabo met Zanele Dlamini, who had grown up in Alexandra township in Johannesburg, and to whom he was introduced in London by Adelaide Tambo. Zanele was Adelaide's relative through marriage. She had obtained a bachelor's degree in social work from the University of the Witwatersrand, before graduating with a diploma in social policy and administration from the London School of Economics and Political Science (LSE) in 1968. She and Thabo were to marry in 1974. Three years Mbeki's elder, Zanele would later become the homemaker and main breadwinner of the family in exile.

In February 1969 the SACP central committee sent Thabo – who had contributed as a member of the editorial board to the party's journal, the *African Communist* – to spend nearly two years studying at the Lenin Institute in Moscow, and then undertaking military training in advanced guerrilla warfare. Both of Mbeki's parents had been members of the Communist Party, and communism of the Soviet variety was thus a longstanding ideological influence. In the Soviet Union Thabo learned to use a gun for the first time in his life, taking courses in managing guerrilla groups, underground organisation, radio communications, explosives, security and intelligence.

It was in Moscow in June 1970 that the 28-year-old Mbeki joined the South African Communist Party (SACP) central committee, along with Chris Hani, who was to become a major rival. The SACP was the home of many of the South African liberation movement's intellectual elite, and Mbeki was therefore attracted to it both ideologically and intellectually. The Soviet Union was also the ANC's largest international funder, and Soviet communism was the orthodoxy of many of its leading members. While at the Lenin Institute Thabo immersed himself in the principles of Leninist vanguardism and 'democratic centralism'. His subjects at the institute included philosophy, political economy, theory and tactics, Soviet history and social psychology. This broad education in Moscow, added to his studies at Sussex, would provide Mbeki with a well-rounded knowledge of both Western and Eastern political economy, and allowed him to maintain a polyglot intellectual identity. In Moscow, his personal political ambitions seem to have been undimmed: it was reported by some of the Canadian students at the institute that Thabo kept telling them that he would become South Africa's first post-apartheid black leader.[2]

Despite his military training, members of the ANC's military wing, Umkhonto we Sizwe, would later belittle Mbeki's lack of military prowess, and regard him as more of a theoretical intellectual than a liberation fighter, someone who was more comfortable with a pen than a pistol. When he was posted to Swaziland in the mid-1970s on a military mission, some of Mbeki's comrades, like Mac Maharaj, were critical of what they regarded as Thabo's lack of success in building an underground movement. Matters built up into a public confrontation in which Maharaj complained that on taking over from Mbeki he had been left with an 'empty folder' of the latter's activities in Swaziland. Maharaj later implied that Thabo had been removed from his post in Swaziland because he lacked the 'personality' for front-line operational management.[3]

Such incidents reinforced perceptions of Mbeki as more of a political than a military leader, who had in any case never spent time in the ANC's military camps. Some military cadres vowed never to be led by him, though many, including Chris Hani, had great respect for his intellect. Other references to him are also revealing of the way in which he was perceived in the exile movement. Consistent with our earlier depiction of Mbeki's monarchical tendencies, he was nicknamed 'the Duke of Kabulonga', after the leafy suburb in Lusaka in which he at one time lived. Some also referred to the dapper dresser as a 'Gucci revolutionary'.[4] Despite these animadversions, Mbeki's work in Swaziland undoubtedly helped to open the path for smuggling South African students out of the country, especially after the Soweto uprising in 1976.

The other ANC cadre of his generation who matched him in promise and stature was Chris Hani, who had been elected with Thabo to the central committee of the SACP at the same age of 28. Hani and Mbeki had been born 10 days apart and about 100 kilometres from each other in the Eastern Cape in June 1942. Both had studied at Lovedale (though Hani was ahead of Mbeki in class), where they shifted allegiance from other youth groups to the ANC Youth League. Both were Renaissance men who devoured Western literary classics: Hani particularly loved the works of Homer, Sophocles and Euripides. He was also greatly influenced by his rival's father, Govan Mbeki, who, like him, was an alumnus of Fort Hare University College.

Unlike Mbeki, Hani was both an intellectual and a soldier: he led the ANC's Luthuli Detachment into Rhodesia in 1967, and, after evading capture by the Rhodesian army, fled to Botswana, where he was arrested and spent time in a Botswana jail. In the mid-1980s Hani was prominent in leading the MK's targeted assassination of apartheid collaborators such as black police officers and community councillors. While Mbeki began to champion a negotiated settlement at this time, Hani continued to push for the prosecution of the armed struggle,[5] though he did attend a meeting with white South African business leaders in Lusaka in 1985. He was, however, distrustful of Mbeki's leadership of these secret talks.[6] Unlike the discreet and tactful Mbeki, Hani was outspoken, accusing the ANC leadership of nepotism for sending their sons to universities in Western Europe in preparation for taking over leadership posts in South Africa after the foot soldiers from non-elite families had overthrown the apartheid government. He dismissed the ANC Youth and Students section, which was at one time led by Mbeki, as 'bogus', and derided those like Thabo in the ANC headquarters in Lusaka as 'armchair revolutionaries'.[7] This rivalry did not stop both men from going together on a ten-day vacation with their wives to the Black Sea resort of Sochi in July 1988.

Mbeki also famously clashed with the SACP stalwart and key ANC strategist, Joe Slovo, who remained a close ideological soul-mate of Chris Hani. Slovo was sent by the SACP central committee to Moscow to discipline Mbeki while he was at the Lenin Institute over an unspecified incident regarding Thabo's conduct towards a woman. This episode reportedly damaged their relationship irreparably.[8] After Slovo criticised Mbeki for an article he had written on China in the *African Communist* in 1972, Thabo left its editorial board and never wrote for the journal again. Despite these difficulties, both Mbeki and Slovo served on the SACP's seven-member Politburo, created in 1977. In the 1980s Slovo saw Mbeki as opportunistically using the ANC's opening to the West to push for the adoption of a centrist social democracy; while Mbeki regarded Slovo's doctrinaire efforts to declare the ANC a socialist organisation as suicidally unrealistic. Thabo once reportedly told a confidant that Slovo did not like him because he had rejected the older man's offer of mentorship.[9] What Mbeki consistently objected to was the patronising arrogance of many white ANC and SACP members who he felt wanted to assume leadership positions rather than remain as ordinary members.

The SACP boss used Thabo's absence from an SACP Politburo meeting in 1982 to drop him from the party's highest decision-making structure, before Thabo was reinstated two years later following an outcry from other party members. Mbeki unsuccessfully opposed Slovo's election to the SACP chair in 1984, noting that a liberated South Africa would not countenance a white president. In a public confrontation, Slovo condemned Mbeki's views as racist. Mbeki – who was himself consistently sceptical of the ANC's military abilities to defeat the apartheid state – grew increasingly wary of Slovo's and Hani's insurrectionist militancy, correctly reading the international environment in the mid-1980s as having become more conducive to a negotiated settlement. In keeping with his political pragmatism and calculating caution, Thabo remained a member of the SACP until 1990.[10] The 'man for all seasons' continued to watch closely which way the political wind was blowing before nailing his colours to the mast and quietly abandoning the SACP on his return to South Africa.

* * *

In April 1971 Thabo Mbeki returned to Africa from London for the first time in nearly a decade. He would work for the ANC on the continent for the next two decades until his return home in April 1990, serving at the ANC headquarters in Zambia, as well as in Swaziland, Botswana and Nigeria. It is important to stress that Mbeki's two-decades-long path to power ran directly through Africa, and not through Europe. In the process, he developed great respect for African solidarity and gratitude for continental support of South Africa's liberation struggle. It was also during this period that Thabo directly witnessed some of the political and socio-economic challenges of post-colonial Africa which he would have to tackle as president.

In Africa he was joined by his wife. In 1971 Zanele won a scholarship to start a doctorate on social welfare – focused on the status of black women under apartheid – at Brandeis University in Boston, though she would never complete it. She was widely respected within the ANC as an intellectual with independent and radical views, and was elected to ANC Women's League positions when the couple lived in Lusaka. She returned to Zambia from the United States to set up the family home in 1974, working for the largely Swedish-funded International University Education Fund (IUEF), which sourced scholarships for black South Africans, until its deputy director, Craig Williamson, was exposed as an apartheid spy. A three-bedroom terraced house on Martin Luther King Close in the Lusaka suburb of Kabulonga became the Mbeki family home for the next two decades. The couple were said to be very private. They spent much time apart because of Thabo's political activism and Zanele's equally busy schedule.

After returning home from exile in 1990, Zanele decided to set up the Women's Development Bank – a micro-enterprise project to support poor women – rather than join ANC party structures. Her devotion to her husband was again evidenced when in the mid-1990s she put her doctorate on hold for a second time to support Thabo's political ambitions. She managed the family's finances and had the foresight to invest in property in Johannesburg following their return to South Africa. After Mbeki assumed the presidency in 1999, she kept a low profile as 'first lady', refusing requests for interviews.[11]

Returning to Africa from European exile in 1971, Thabo served as the assistant to Moses Mabhida, the secretary of the ANC's newly established Revolutionary Council, a body whose task was to get MK soldiers back into South Africa. Exile was not an easy place to be: the ANC had been expelled for a time from Tanzania, while their Zambian hosts were ambivalent about their presence, restricting their activities for fear of provoking a military response from the apartheid regime. In Zambia the ANC built up a sizeable infrastructure, and would eventually build up a sizeable army in Angola by 1990. But further problems were created for the ANC when Mozambique signed the US-brokered Nkomati Accord with Pretoria in March 1984, in a further betrayal of the anti-apartheid struggle, as the ANC had to withdraw its military leadership and hundreds of cadres from this strategic country and neighbour of South Africa. In 1989, as part of a superpower-brokered deal to end the Angolan civil war, thousands of ANC fighters were also forced to leave that country for camps in Uganda. While exiles like Mbeki were grateful for African support for their liberation struggle, these actions of the Front Line States must also have rankled and created some resentment.

* * *

Mbeki spent most of 1973 and 1974 in Botswana, working with the government and cultivating links with the Black Consciousness Movement in South Africa. He joined the ANC's most powerful decision-making body – the National Executive Committee (NEC) – in January 1975, shortly before being dispatched to Swaziland and a year before the apartheid state would kill at least 176 protesting students in Soweto and step up its internal repression and external attacks on its African neighbours. Thabo's rival, Chris Hani, joined the NEC at the same time, just as they had joined the SACP central committee together. While Mbeki ran ANC operations out of the tiny kingdom of Swaziland, travelling often to Mozambique after that country's independence in 1975, Hani performed the same job from the Lilliputian mountain kingdom of Lesotho. It was a dangerous time for the ANC: South African double agents were ubiquitous in exile, and apartheid security forces killed ANC operatives in Lesotho (42 people in a December 1982 raid) as well as in Botswana and Mozambique. These threats were clear and ever-present, and must have contributed to a heightened sense of fear and suspicion, even paranoia.

The disruption and dislocation that the Mbeki family endured in these times was symptomatic of the larger tragedy that befell many black political families during the liberation struggle. With her husband in jail for life, Thabo's mother, Epainette, struggled financially and had to close her shop, moving to another village in the Eastern Cape. Epainette visited her husband, Govan, only twice in the 23 years that he spent on Robben Island: in 1965 and in 1981. Upon his release in 1987, Govan did not move back to the Transkei to join her, but went to live in Port Elizabeth. While on Robben Island, Govan wrote to Thabo only twice: once to urge him to act as a parent to his younger brothers, and another after his youngest brother, Jama, had disappeared in 1982.[12]

This lack of paternal connection must have toughened Mbeki but would also have been emotionally hurtful. During this period, the Mbekis suffered another personal tragedy when Jama, the youngest sibling, who had been working as a lawyer in Botswana, was arrested in March 1982 on charges of fraud and accessory to murder, having reportedly agreed somewhat naively to take part in an ANC underground operation against suspected apartheid agents. Thabo arranged for bail to be paid for his brother, for whom he had earlier arranged a scholarship to study law at Leeds University. However, the day before Jama was to appear in court, he fled to Lesotho, where he was most likely killed by the country's security forces.[13]

In Swaziland, Thabo Mbeki worked with his deputy, Albert Dhlomo, to recruit young black South African activists, many steeped in the radical Black Consciousness of Steve Biko that had swept the black school and university campuses in the late 1960s and early 1970s rather than the moderate 'non-racialism' of the ANC. Many of these activists would leave South Africa and secure places to study in Botswana, Lesotho and Swaziland, and were to form the core of a new generation of recruits who would help revive the dormant ANC. Thabo maintained a high profile for an underground operative, and was well known on the Swazi social scene. He also attracted South African student admirers, and helped to recruit many students into the ANC in Swaziland.[14] Mbeki also worked closely, from 1976, with Jacob Zuma, forging a close relationship with the man who would later become his deputy president and eventually oust him from power in September 2008. Zuma was in charge of the ANC underground responsible for recruiting fighters from Natal province. He had spent ten years on Robben Island between 1963 and 1973 shortly after he joined Umkhonto we Sizwe. Both Mbeki and Zuma spent some time in Swaziland's Mastapha maximum security prison in 1976 after pressure was placed on Swazi authorities by the apartheid state. They narrowly escaped being repatriated to South Africa and instead made their way to the newly independent state of Mozambique.

As we have seen, the ANC's presence in the Front Line States was not assured. ANC operatives were arrested in Botswana, and underground MK soldiers were jailed and tortured in Zimbabwe (in 1982). After Angola's independence in 1975 and its collapse into a decades-long civil war between the rival MPLA, UNITA and the FNLA, Zambia's and Tanzania's support for a united front of liberation movements in Angola strained relations with the ANC, which was strongly pro-MPLA. Zambia at one stage shut down the ANC's Radio Freedom broadcasts, while Tanzania became increasingly averse to hosting MK camps, which impelled the MK to set up facilities in Angola.[15] These developments all shaped Mbeki's understanding of the potential ambivalence, shifting nature and even duplicity of pan-African diplomacy. Though a pragmatic Marxist pan-African in the mould of Nkrumah, Mbeki took to heart many of the lessons learned from these African experiences. While African governments all pledged rhetorical support to South Africa's liberation struggle, many also promoted more parochial, short-term interests while some – above all, Mozambique – were forced to bow to apartheid pressure. Guided by Oliver Tambo, Thabo adopted an approach of diversifying the ANC's dependence without becoming over-reliant on African governments.

* * *

After being deported from Swaziland by the authorities, Mbeki was 'deployed' to establish an ANC office in Africa's most populous country, Nigeria, in December 1976. This was to be funded by the Nigerian military administration of General Olusegun Obasanjo. His stay in Nigeria would be a formative experience that resulted in the emergence of Thabo's most important strategic alliance when he became president in 1999. From this first-hand experience, South Africa's future president developed a great admiration for Nigeria's sense of fierce independence, its irrepressible intellectual culture, and its aggressive indigenous capitalist class. Zanele moved with her husband to Nigeria to spend most of 1977 in Lagos. This was particularly convenient, as most of the South African scholars that she was overseeing through the IUEF had been placed in Nigerian institutions of higher learning.

Mbeki headed the ANC delegation to attend Nigeria's lavish Festival of Arts and Culture (FESTAC) in 1977, involving 70,000 delegates from 50 countries from Africa and its diaspora. Among other things he went to social weddings and funerals; devoured the vibrant press and rich literature; marvelled at the country's entrepreneurial spirit; was astonished by its socio-economic divisions; admired the radical anti-establishment Nigerian musician Fela Anikulapo-Kuti, whose 'Afrika Shrine' club he visited in Lagos; watched the popular television series *Village Headmaster*; and interacted closely with key senior officials, including his former Sussex classmate, Baba Gana Kingibe, who served as a political aide to the military head of state, as well as the radical intellectual Yusuf Bala Usman. Thabo also visited Nigerian universities to spread the gospel of the anti-apartheid struggle, and was instrumental in making a success of the UN Conference for Action Against Apartheid which was hosted in Lagos in 1977.

Nigeria built one of Africa's few genuinely grassroots anti-apartheid movements with the Southern African Relief Fund. With chapters nationwide, it was established in 1976 to provide South Africans with scholarships to Nigerian institutions of learning (400 black South African students arrived in the country a year later). Nigerian public servants also had a 'Mandela tax' automatically deducted from their monthly salaries to support South Africa's liberation struggle. FESTAC had a profound influence on the ANC in promoting groups such as the cast of the musical *Ipi Tombi* and the Amandla Cultural Ensemble to tour the world in a bid to increase awareness of the anti-apartheid struggle.[16]

Mbeki clearly recognised the huge importance of Nigeria for Africa. As he later noted, 'It's an extraordinary society, an African society. It doesn't have this big imprint of colonial oppression. It's something else. Very different from here [South Africa]. You get a sense that you are now really being exposed to the real Africa, not where *we* come from … they do their own thing. [And] they are of such importance on the African continent that they could mislead lots of people.' Mark Gevisser's depiction of Mbeki's reaction to Nigeria is particularly interesting: 'Mbeki is not an "outside observer": he has crossed over into the "real Africa" as other South Africans have not. And yet his relationship to this "real Africa", of which he has been made a citizen, is fraught with ambivalence, for with every example he presents, it becomes clearer that even though he is attracted to it, it is antithetical to everything he stands for.'[17]

This fascinating observation suggests that Mbeki was somewhat alienated from his African roots and reveals his ambivalent relationship to his ancestral continent. Though an instinctive pan-African intellectually, he is also an acculturated Englishman. When he came face to face with what he himself clumsily described as the 'real Africa', Mbeki needed to make some adjustment to it, and did not seem totally comfortable with what he encountered. These observations on his path to power are important to bear in mind, as Thabo would often borrow lessons from Europe, North America and Asia while in office as president rather than from Africa. One also needs to remember that when he became deputy president and then president of South Africa, he was ruling a strange country from which he had been away for three decades.

Mbeki often felt that Nigeria's lack of a white settler history made the political rulers in Lagos impatient in their understanding of the ANC's need to accommodate South African whites. He was irritated by the frustration of Obasanjo's military administration with what it regarded as the ANC's lacklustre conduct of the 'armed struggle' (urging them to 'go home and fight!'). This was a frustration that many MK soldiers themselves felt. Mbeki was also annoyed by Nigeria's insistence on and backing for a common front of the ANC, the break-away Pan Africanist Congress (PAC), and the Soweto Students' Representative Council (SSRC).[18] During his time in Lagos, Thabo was successful in establishing the ANC's pre-eminence among South Africa's liberation movements in the country.

* * *

Oliver Tambo had been sent into exile in 1960 by the ANC president, Albert Luthuli, to ensure that the movement could continue if its internal leadership was arrested. Following Luthuli's death in July 1967, Tambo had become ANC president. After leaving Nigeria in early 1978, the 36-year-old Thabo Mbeki became Tambo's political secretary, based in Lusaka. At this time, the ANC-in-exile had an annual budget of $56 million; controlled several military camps in Africa; supported a school in Tanzania; sponsored over 1,000 students on scholarship; and owned two large farms.[19] As his secretary, Thabo drafted Tambo's speeches and the ANC's major public documents, and became the ANC president's trusted confidant. He would later recall that he felt embarrassed when in the early days the perfectionist 'O.R.' would reject his draft speeches and use his own notes to deliver his speech. Tambo spent hours patiently explaining to his young protégé why some of Thabo's formulations were too careless or imprecise to be used, training him in the process in the subtleties of the ANC's history, values and traditions.[20] This experience would make Mbeki himself a perfectionist in his own work.

Through his closeness to Tambo and the trust that his political mentor had in him, Thabo was levered, perhaps he even manoeuvred himself, into a powerful position.[21] He was not just a gatekeeper, but, because Tambo travelled so often, some saw him as the *de facto* head of the ANC in the absence of the astute chief. This earned Mbeki the unflattering sobriquet of the 'national interferer'. Thabo developed a Machiavellian reputation among some for manipulative cunning, and was accused of often hiding behind Tambo to wield 'power without authority'.

The relationship between the two men was undoubtedly crucial in Mbeki's meteoric rise to power. The soft-spoken Tambo, widely acknowledged to be a man of great humility and impeccable integrity, was more than a father-figure for Thabo: he was, in a sense, the father he never had. Tambo, like Mbeki, had the mannerisms of an English gentleman. He was renowned for being a perfectionist and maintained an impressive work ethic.

He was also a consummate strategist, and was credited with keeping together, and securing widespread support for, Africa's oldest liberation movement under the most difficult and pressured circumstances in exile. Mbeki imbibed many of his political mentor's traits, and, when in charge as deputy president and then president of South Africa, insisted on drafting every important document and speech himself. Some even felt that Thabo had adopted some of Tambo's mannerisms of being polite, humble and always ready to listen (responding only after everyone had spoken), as well as providing moderate responses.[22] Mbeki carried the habit of being reluctant to delegate into his presidency, where a style for micromanagement proved harmful, as cabinet members felt disempowered and regarded the president as intolerant of dissent.[23]

Mbeki became a consummate diplomat, the chief spokesman and salesman for the ANC in exile. In 1985 he was appointed to head the party's Department of Information and Publicity (previously, Propaganda). In this role, he oversaw some of the party's publications such as *Sechaba* and its Radio Freedom. He also courted liberal South African journalists and influential Western media.[24] He was astute enough to understand the importance of these actors in raising public awareness about, and winning public support for, the anti-apartheid struggle. Mbeki's agreement to allow an American film-crew to make a documentary about the ANC – in the teeth of vehement opposition from other comrades – and his published articles in prominent Western newspapers like the *New York Times* and the *Washington Post* fuelled further envy and suspicion within the liberation movement. An unfounded allegation that Thabo was a US Central Intelligence Agency (CIA) operative was particularly irksome, and underlined the climate of paranoia and the threat of 'dirty tricks' that infested political exile.[25] But Mbeki understood well the significance of public relations to his cause, and the showing of the 1978 CBS documentary *The Battle for South Africa* was the first time that a mainstream American audience would have the opportunity to view the ANC as a legitimate liberation struggle movement rather than as armed terrorists. It would help give credibility to the anti-apartheid campaign in America, which eventually secured the imposition of economic sanctions by Congress against South Africa in 1986, with Republicans joining Democrats to override President Ronald Reagan's reactionary veto.

Mbeki was disparaging about the ANC's military achievements, noting in a confidential report to Tambo in 1978: 'It is said correctly that one should judge a lion by its claws rather than its roar. We must admit among ourselves that our roar is indeed very thunderous while our claws are virtually absent.'[26] As Joe Slovo himself admitted, by 1975 the ANC had not fired a single shot in anger at the apartheid state inside South Africa for

14 years.[27] Thabo's early push for a negotiated settlement with the Afrikaner-dominated National Party would lead to accusations that his search for a political solution was the result of his own lack of military prowess. His closeness to Swedish diplomats (he started visiting Stockholm in 1974), who generously supported the ANC, raised further suspicion among some of his comrades that he was more comfortable with Nordic 'social democracy' than with Soviet communism. But Mbeki's goal was to pursue self-determination through Stockholm in order to avoid clientelism under Moscow.[28] His embrace of Swedish social democracy was also reportedly influenced by Oliver Tambo,[29] who had formed a particularly close relationship with the Swedish premier Olof Palme, who was assassinated in 1986, some say by South African agents. He remained antagonistic towards Communist China until after the end of the Cold War, and also adopted a lukewarm attitude towards Fidel Castro's Cuba.[30]

Thabo was often an independent and strategic thinker. At an ANC meeting in Zambia in 1988, he questioned the efficacy of nationalisation, a sacred cow of ANC economic policy at the time. Mbeki argued that the nationalisation of copper mines in the movement's host country, under Kenneth Kaunda, had been catastrophic for Zambia's economy.[31] In 1990 he would give up his membership of the South African Communist Party not only because of ideological disagreements with Joe Slovo, but also because of his reading of the international climate after the fall of the Berlin Wall in 1989 and the failure of Mikhail Gorbachev's policy of perestroika, which eventually culminated in the collapse of the Soviet Union in 1991. Thabo often kept his options open, pushing for a negotiated settlement to end apartheid, while not completely ruling out armed struggle.

As a globe-trotting ANC diplomat, Mbeki's friendships were often 'instrumentalist and expedient'.[32] He openly championed non-alignment, derived from India's founding prime minister, Jawaharlal Nehru, to keep a distance from the two superpower blocs of the Cold War period, while promoting an independent role for his party in world politics. This was a difficult position to maintain for as long as Moscow continued to be the ANC's largest funder (Nehru's India itself was effectively in a *de facto* military alliance with Moscow). It soon became clear with the arrival of Gorbachev in the Kremlin in March 1985 that Moscow could abandon the ANC if its policy of glasnost and rapprochement with the West bore fruit. Non-alignment thus became less an aspiration than a necessity.

Mbeki started to visit the US regularly from the early 1980s. A close ally in the ANC, Johnny Makatini, had set up the organisation's New York office in the 1970s, and Thabo assiduously courted America's liberal establishment. The fact that Oliver Tambo took only Mbeki with him into his meeting with Gorbachev in Moscow in November 1986 (though Joe Slovo and Chris

Hani had also travelled with the delegation) was another clear sign to many that Tambo had anointed Mbeki as his successor as ANC president. Two months later, the ANC chief again took his young protégé to Washington to meet, for the first time, the US secretary of state, George Shultz. The imposition by the superpowers of a peace agreement to secure Namibia's independence under effective UN 'trusteeship' in 1989–90 would reinforce Mbeki's belief in the need to avoid becoming a pawn on the chessboard of the superpowers, and made him more determined to pursue a home-grown solution for South Africa's democratic transition.[33]

* * *

In the mid-1980s South Africa declined into virtual civil war, as the black townships erupted in protest at apartheid. At first, the 'mass action' revolts were met by the imposition of a state of emergency, which involved widespread repression, arrest and torture by apartheid security forces. Especially after international opinion began to turn decisively against the regime and the major international banks refused to extend credit to it, the government of P.W. Botha soon began to look for a way out and initiated talks with the jailed Nelson Mandela from 1985.

In the lead-up to negotiations to end apartheid between 1987 and 1990 (the 'talks about talks'), Thabo Mbeki was centrally involved in a series of meetings, some in secret, in Africa, Europe and the US to reassure white South African politicians, businessmen and academics that the ANC would run the country in a responsible manner and not seek retribution against its former oppressors. Thabo led an ANC delegation to the Senegalese capital of Dakar in July 1987 to meet a group of Afrikaners, who were charmed by his manner, though at least two of them, Frederik van Zyl Slabbert and Max du Preez, would later criticise Thabo's cunning manipulation and ruthless leadership as president.[34] Chris Hani strongly opposed these talks when he found out about them, arguing that the armed struggle needed to be stepped up to give the ANC greater leverage, and warning that black South Africans could perceive the negotiations as selling out their struggle.[35]

Always wanting to keep his options open, Mbeki chaired an SACP congress in the Cuban capital of Havana in April 1989. The congress adopted the Joe Slovo-inspired document 'The Path to Power', which championed a 'seizure of power' through 'mass insurrection'. Not wanting to be isolated by the left wing of his movement, Mbeki pursued what he described as 'parallel paths to power' even as he was convinced by his negotiations with white interest groups of the imminent defeat of the insurrectionary path.[36] In September 1989 Mbeki and Jacob Zuma travelled to the Swiss town of Lucerne for the first formal meeting of the ANC-in-exile with South African government officials. Mbeki also travelled tirelessly to meet with members of

South Africa's business community at country estates and other locations in England in gatherings funded by the mining giant Consolidated Goldfields. (The Nigerian-British actor Chiwetel Ejiofor skilfully depicted Mbeki's suave diplomacy during these meetings in the 2009 film *Endgame*.) Thabo used his legendary silver tongue and charm to appeal to the 'pioneering spirit' of the Afrikaner groups he met, whom he referred to as 'new Voortrekkers', and argued correctly within ANC structures that it would be easier to defeat a divided enemy – Afrikaner intellectuals, business, politicians and state officials, and securocrats – which had increasing doubts about old certainties.[37] Thabo's engagement in talks for a negotiated settlement was simultaneously being pursued by Mandela in jail, and was eventually accepted as ANC policy in the Harare Declaration of 1989. After its adoption the Zambian president, Kenneth Kaunda, lent Tambo and Mbeki his presidential plane to tour southern Africa to sell the declaration to regional leaders, which they successfully did.

This gruelling tour of southern Africa would contribute to Tambo's debilitating stroke, which he suffered in his Lusaka office in August 1989. He was airlifted to hospital in London where Mbeki was one of his first visitors. During this meeting, Tambo asked Mbeki to look after the ANC and ensure the victory of the liberation movement. He also instructed Thabo to begin communicating with Mandela in jail by telephone.[38] This meeting was touchingly personal, but also represented the symbolic passing of the leadership torch from one generation to the next. Describing Tambo as 'one of the most important founders of democratic South Africa,' Mbeki later commented: 'I am immensely privileged that I had the opportunity to interact with and learn many lifelong lessons from Oliver Tambo during the 31 years from 1962, until he passed away in 1993.'[39] The ANC patriarch's great influence on the movement was evidenced by the fact that during Tambo's absence due to ill health, though Alfred Nzo was nominally in charge of the party, Mbeki struggled to rally support for his negotiation strategy among his party's leadership without O.R.'s presence.[40]

* * *

In January 1990 Govan Mbeki and Walter Sisulu, who had been released from Robben Island, travelled with their wives, Epainette and Albertina, to Lusaka to meet with the ANC-in-exile. In the next month, the recently appointed South African president, F.W. de Klerk, announced the unbanning of the liberation movements and the release of Nelson Mandela from jail.

It is often said that exiles keep journeying but somehow never quite arrive at their destination. It is the kindness of strangers that sustains the nostalgia for home. In April 1990 Thabo Mbeki returned to South Africa for the first time in nearly three decades. In a rare public display of emotion in Cape Town, he stood next to his father and wept, betraying the 'stiff upper lip' self-control and stoicism inculcated by his years of English training.

Even after his return home, Mbeki raised suspicion among some of his comrades, like Joe Slovo and Cyril Ramaphosa (a trade union leader who became ANC secretary-general in 1991), with his close relationship with the white business community, whose members had collaborated closely with apartheid and were now assiduously courting a future black-led government. (It is ironic that Ramaphosa himself would later come to be seen as a major defender of white corporate interests after becoming incredibly wealthy from a career in business upon leaving politics in 1994.) For the first few weeks after his return, Thabo lived in accommodation – an executive suite at the Carlton Court – provided by the South African multinational Anglo American. Members of the corporate world also started to refer to Mbeki as 'our man in the ANC'. [41] Thabo hobnobbed with businessmen like 'Casino King' Sol Kerzner – an alleged sponsor of the leaders of some former Bantustans (homelands) where his casinos had been situated – who reportedly paid for a surprise fiftieth birthday party for Mbeki in June 1992. [42]

At the ANC conference in Durban in July 1991, Mbeki was able – unlike Mandela – to persuade delegates to abandon the call for sanctions against the apartheid regime, arguing that most of the world had lifted them anyway and that the party would lose its leverage in negotiations if it continued to insist on them. [43] This was also the conference at which Chris Hani famously challenged Mbeki for the deputy presidency of the ANC, reportedly remarking to friends: 'If Thabo stands I will stand against him. I will not serve under him. He will sell the ANC down the river.'[44] Party elders eventually persuaded both men to stand down in favour of the octogenarian Walter Sisulu in order to avoid a damaging split in the party on the eve of political negotiations. In elections to the ANC's National Executive Committee in Durban, Chris Hani came first with 94.7 per cent of the votes cast, ahead of Mbeki's 93 per cent. Mbeki won the National Working Committee poll with 66 votes to Hani's 65. At this stage, Jacob Zuma had left the SACP with Mbeki in 1990, and was working closely with him to persuade Mangosuthu Buthelezi's Inkatha Freedom Party (IFP) and potential Afrikaner separatists led by General Constand Viljoen to remain in the peace process. Mbeki also cultivated contacts with the Stellenbosch University academic Willie Esterhuyse and members of the elite Afrikaner secret society, the Broederbond.[45] At this stage Zuma and Aziz Pahad were Thabo's most vocal supporters in the ANC's National Executive Committee.[46]

During the negotiations for South Africa's political transition between 1990 and 1994, Mbeki – having raised suspicions within the ANC following his courting of the Broederbond and being regarded as too much of a moderate, unwilling to resort to the use of 'rolling mass action' to force the pace of negotiations – suffered a setback when his party replaced him as chief negotiator in August 1991 with Cyril Ramaphosa. Mandela's later observation about Mbeki is particularly insightful in this context: 'He would not confront problems directly as I have done. He is too diplomatic for that. He is sometimes criticized by our own people, who say he is indecisive when faced with a situation that requires firmness.'[47] This comment says much about Mbeki's risk-averse, cautious and calculating nature, which would later shape his approach to socio-economic transformation once in power. After being replaced by Ramaphosa as chief negotiator, Thabo went through one of the most difficult periods of his life, until he took over from Oliver Tambo as ANC national chairman in 1993. He then astutely and quietly cultivated the support of Peter Mokaba and Winnie Mandela (the leaders of the ANC Youth and Women's leagues respectively) to build a support base for becoming Mandela's deputy as president in the new democratic government.[48]

In April 1993 – the same month as Oliver Tambo's death – another tragic event would clear Mbeki's last major obstacle to succeeding Mandela as president of the ANC and thus of South Africa. His long-time rival, Chris Hani, was assassinated by a right-wing extremist outside his Johannesburg home. This was the day that Mandela effectively became the country's president, even though F.W. de Klerk had not yet lost power, by making a live television broadcast to calm the nation and urge peace.

If he had not been murdered, many have speculated that the popular and charismatic Chris Hani might well have acceded to the country's presidency instead of Mbeki in June 1999.

4

The domestic president

When the Government of National Unity was formed after the first-ever democratic elections of 1994, Nelson Mandela apparently preferred at first the ANC secretary-general, Cyril Ramaphosa (a man of Venda origin) as deputy, reportedly to avoid another Xhosa – Thabo Mbeki – succeeding him. But party elders led by Walter Sisulu persuaded Mandela to appoint Thabo as his deputy and heir apparent.[1] Mandela also consulted with two African elder statesmen who had worked closely with the ANC-in-exile: Zambia's Kenneth Kaunda and Tanzania's Julius Nyerere, who both supported Mbeki for the position.[2]

Thabo's political godfather, Oliver Tambo, had died in April 1993, removing from the scene one of the ANC's political titans and a powerful supporter of Mbeki's presidential ambitions. At Tambo's funeral in May 1993, Mandela described 'O.R.' as 'a great giant who strode the globe like a colossus'.[3] Mbeki would need the patronage of another ANC grandee to fulfil his ambitions: Nelson Mandela. Just as Thabo had shadowed Tambo as his protégé in African exile, he worked in the background of Mandela as deputy president between 1994 and 1999, effectively running the country with the protection and support of the revered president while preparing for his own formal coronation. Though Mandela was nominally in charge of the country between 1994 and 1999, the septuagenarian patriarch effectively handed over the chairing of cabinet meetings to the two deputy presidents, Mbeki and F.W. de Klerk, and largely served as a ceremonial president, leaving the day-to-day running of the country mainly to Thabo.[4]

Mbeki's relationship with Madiba was a complex one. Both came from the educated Xhosa elite; had attended Christian missionary schools; and were anglophiles who greatly admired British culture and institutions. During the 1980s both seemed instinctively to know when to open negotiations with the apartheid government. Both feared a white right-wing backlash during the transition, and both felt the need to placate white fears in order to maintain stability in the post-apartheid era. Both also often used the royal 'we' when referring to themselves. But while Mandela lived almost all of his life in South Africa, for 27 years of which he was in jail, Mbeki had spent 28 years outside South Africa, in both Europe and Africa. Whereas Mandela ruled like a patriarch, leaving policy

71

details to his lieutenants, Mbeki was a policy wonk who revelled in the details of governance. While Mandela was charismatic and hugely popular among the broad mass of people, Mbeki relied on political manoeuvring and back-room deals within the ANC to operate and stay in power.

There were tensions, too, between the two men in government: Mbeki felt that Mandela treated him like an apprentice, even as he delegated to him the day-to-day administration of the country. He was also irritated by Mandela's decision to take him abroad and introduce him to the world as the great man's successor, after Thabo became ANC president in December 1997.[5]

Mbeki remarked that it was he who kept Mandela on the path of constitutional legality, noting that Madiba often lacked the listening abilities and consultative approach of Oliver Tambo. As Thabo complained to his confidants, 'This is not the way O.R. would have done it. Where is the wisdom of O.R. when we need it?'[6] As president, Mbeki felt slighted by Mandela's calling on the US president, Bill Clinton, in the White House just days before Mbeki's first state visit to Washington in May 2000. The tension between the two men was such that Mbeki sometimes refused to take his predecessor's telephone calls.

Mbeki inevitably struggled to emerge from the shadow of his saintly predecessor, and often complained about 'Mandela exceptionalism' and the 'one good native' syndrome: the anxiety prior to Mandela's departure from office that Madiba was the only good leader who could come out of Africa, and that South Africa would slide into chaos like the rest of the continent once he had left power.[7] Mandela won international acclaim for his preaching of national reconciliation, which may, in retrospect, have done damage to the country by failing to hold whites to account for their role in colluding with apartheid. Mbeki, in contrast, seemed to many observers to abandon his predecessor's inclusive vision of forgiveness and reconciliation when he sought to force his country's citizens to confront their racist past and start to redress the historical injustices that still left South Africa's black majority at the bottom of the socio-economic ladder in one of the world's most unequal societies.

Yet Mbeki's fiery rhetoric would not be matched with radical action in the field of social and economic policy. Even given the clear domestic and external constraints faced by an ANC government, there were many paradoxes in this situation. Why did Mbeki, a trained Marxist development economist and consummate political operator, not make a more radical analysis of the inherited contradictions of the apartheid state and take decisive action to transform the socio-economic conditions of the black masses? Why did he retreat so quickly into cautious neo-liberal orthodoxy? Why was he so keen to win credibility from domestic and foreign business interests even in the face of policies that clearly were not achieving their desired outcomes?

Mbeki assumed the ANC presidency at the party's

conference in Mafikeng in December 1997. He and his
supporters were able to have Jacob Zuma appointed as
his deputy, confident that this man of limited education
and lack of open political ambition would pose no threat
to him as a successor.[8] In Mafikeng, Mandela praised
his heir's brilliance but warned ominously: 'One of the
temptations of a leader who has been elected unopposed
is that he may use his powerful position to settle scores
with his detractors, marginalise them, and, in certain
cases, get rid of them and surround himself with yes-men
and -women.'[9] Madiba also issued another unmistakable
caution to his deputy: 'The leader must keep the forces
together, but you can't do that unless you allow dissent.
People should be able to criticise the leader without fear
or favour. Only in that case are you likely to keep your
colleagues together.'[10]

Mbeki would gain his own revenge during a speech
at Mandela's eightieth birthday in July 1998. In a light-
hearted but needling address, Thabo compared South
Africa's avuncular president to Shakespeare's King Lear,
remarking that Madiba was planning a rural retirement
'to tell old tales and laugh at gilded butterflies, and hear
poor rogues talk of court news'.[11] Some read this as a
reference to an autocratic, senile leader retreating into
retirement and old age. Mandela later criticised ANC
members at a National Working Committee meeting
for not standing up to Mbeki, even when they knew he
was wrong.[12] The nadir of their relationship was reached

in March 2002 at an ANC meeting at which Mbeki's supporters humiliated Mandela for having spoken out against the government's damaging HIV/AIDS policies in public, outside party structures. It would be the last such meeting that Mandela attended.

* * *

As a political figure, Thabo Mbeki was a man of great complexity. He was notoriously shy and conflict-averse, but yet ruled with deft and shrewd adroitness. His short physique led to accusations of a 'Napoleon complex', consistent with the notion of monarchical rule. Yet Mbeki remained a constitutional monarch who never drifted into autocracy and always observed the constitutional limits during his eight years in office. Mandela – one of the twentieth century's greatest moral figures – had used his incredible charisma as a leader to provide political stability, legitimacy and credibility to the 'new' South Africa's fledgling institutions. Mbeki, on the other hand, built his support and power base around a group of trusted loyalists, many, though not all, of whom had been in exile with him: Essop and Aziz Pahad, Joel Netshitenzhe, Sydney Mufamadi, Joe Modise, Charles Nqakula, Sam Shilowa, Jabu Moleketi, Geraldine Fraser-Moleketi, Nkosazana Dlamini-Zuma, Phumzile Mlambo-Ngcuka, Smuts Ngonyama, Frank Chikane, Trevor Manuel, Tito Mboweni and Alec Erwin.[13] Essop Pahad, minister in the presidency, a close Mbeki confidant and the best man at his wedding, was a particularly important figure. Some saw him as playing the role of *de facto* prime minister and enforcer for Mbeki, sometimes snapping at government critics like a pit bull terrier.

In power, the intensely private Mbeki was considered by many of his critics to be aloof and arrogant. Some of his supporters described this more as shyness and reticence than arrogance.[14] Others regarded him as a scheming Machiavellian figure who brooked no dissent, ruthlessly co-opted or eliminated political rivals through smear campaigns, and surrounded himself with mediocre allies who would not challenge him. Thomas Nkobi, at one time ANC treasurer-general, once characterised Thabo as a leader who surrounded himself with fools, adding in jest: 'He is the chief, all the others are Indians.'[15] This was the 'Prince' to Kwame Nkrumah's 'King'.

From his university days in England between 1962 and 1966, Mbeki had developed an admiration for the British political culture of pragmatism and of 'muddling through'. This approach favoured stability over disorder, and an evolutionary rather than revolutionary path to change. But it was also a system that stored up larger structural problems for the future. Under Mbeki's administration, inequality actually increased, and sectors such as health, education, the civil service and local government were not transformed sufficiently to lift the poor black majority out of their inherited misery. Despite Mbeki's rhetoric insisting on a transformation of

South Africa's institutions, the major government-funded universities – the traditional sites for the production of knowledge and waging intellectual debates – remained spectacularly untransformed both racially (at faculty level) and intellectually (at the curriculum level). Many white-dominated institutions continued to lack a pan-African awareness or identification with their African roots. As the Ugandan scholar Mahmood Mamdani noted after a frustrating stint at the University of Cape Town between 1996 and 1999, an African Renaissance could not take place without an Africa-focused intelligentsia.[16]

Mbeki formally succeeded Mandela as president of South Africa in June 1999, after a general election in which the ANC won 66.3 per cent of the vote, a two-thirds majority that could have enabled the ruling party to change the Constitution. In running his administration, Thabo appears to have taken the Leninist idea of 'democratic centralism' to heart, with the executive using the ANC-dominated parliament in effect as a rubber-stamp. Much policy and coordination was centralised in the Presidency. The workaholic Mbeki was widely considered to be a micro-manager, who, as president, insisted on appointing provincial premiers and top civil servants, and centralised power in an executive with over 300 staff. Kader Asmal, Mbeki's education minister between 1999 and 2004, offered an insider perspective: 'Cabinet carried on with the day-to-day business of governance and the managing of our individual portfolios, but the difficult, controversial decisions, strategising and policy formulation took place within the rapidly expanding Office of the President.'[17] The veteran ANC member and former parliamentarian Ben Turok similarly noted: 'the Presidency became increasingly dominant in the work of government. As a consequence, the ANC as a party found itself distanced from major policy and decision-making processes. In turn, Parliament itself became less democratic and participatory.'[18]

Within the cabinet, Kader Asmal painted a picture of a perfectionist Mbeki paying incredible attention to detail, reading every document meticulously, but he also observed: 'As the months went by in Mbeki's first term as President, a climate bordering on anxiety began to settle on the Cabinet. It was suddenly difficult to raise issues because you were unsure what kind of response there would be. You started to think very carefully about which battles to fight and which to let slide. As a minister, you very rarely made any assessment or criticism of Mbeki, if you could help it. You never knew what the response would be. We practised the injunction *maak toe jou mond* (shut your mouth). But I don't think this climate of silence and obedience within the executive branch of our new democracy was established consciously. All the same, it was not very healthy.'[19]

Mbeki also sought to reach grassroots communities through *imbizos* in which he traversed the country listening to ordinary citizens' problems while taking copious notes. In addition, he convened twice-yearly cabinet *lekgotlas* at which ministers and directors-general of state departments were required to present concrete goals and measurable achievements. Nevertheless, under Mbeki's administration, there was also evidence of poor performance by some of his ministers, who sometimes failed to attend parliamentary caucuses as they were constitutionally obliged to do. Cadre deployment was another major criticism of the ANC government, with state positions being allocated to party members of increasingly lower calibre.[20] Whereas portfolio committee chairs, parliamentary whips and other positions in the South African parliament had traditionally been filled through election in the past, these posts came to be determined through a process of cadre deployment directed from the ANC headquarters in Luthuli House. Ben Turok described one incident during Mbeki's first year in office when an independent economist criticised the government's economic policies while providing a briefing to members of the parliamentary committee on financial policy. Upon learning about this presentation, Mbeki summoned the ANC members of the committee to his office, where he expressed strong concern at the finance committee having been used to criticise government policy.[21] This was clearly not the action of an intellectual open to diverse views that could strengthen policy formulation, but a stern and intimidating political operator.

The reported discovery in April 2001 of a 'plot' against Mbeki by three political rivals – Cyril Ramaphosa, Mathews Phosa and Tokyo Sexwale – as publicly announced by the minister of safety and security, Steve Tshwete, was seen by many as a paranoid carry-over of ANC political culture into the democratic order. At an NEC meeting that discussed the plot, Pallo Jordan was one of the few people to challenge the idea, arguing that as long as individuals sought to oust a president through ANC structures, it was legitimate to do so. Nearly 15 years later, in January 2016, Mbeki sought to explain this incident away by noting that an ANC Youth League leader, James Nkambule, had provided his government with information about a plot to harm the presidency, for which no evidence could be found after a government investigation. Mbeki described Tshwete's public naming of the three accused men as a 'serious mistake' and noted that he had reprimanded him.[22] But two obvious questions remain: Why had Mbeki not sacked his minister for such a serious allegation that cast aspersions on three innocent individuals without any credible evidence? And, why has Mbeki himself never apologised to his three comrades for a false allegation by his administration? (Both Tshwete and Nkambule later apologised to the three men.) Mbeki's 'rule by plot' was more common of autocratic leaders like Guinea's Sékou Touré, who used it in a more sinister way to eliminate political rivals such as the widely respected first secretary-general of the Organisation of African Unity, Diallo Telli.

Others would also feel the brunt of Mbeki's wrath. As the former president recalled in January 2016, the SACP deputy general secretary, Jeremy Cronin, had engaged in 'fabrications' when he told an Irish academic, Helena Sheehan, in a private interview, that 'there is bullying of the left' and warned of the 'Zanufication of the ANC'.[23] As the deputy general secretary recalled, following this incident Mbeki's allies publicly dismissed Cronin as a 'white messiah' and a snake in the grass whose head needed to be crushed. Cronin then faced an orchestrated grilling by the ANC's NEC in August 2002 for a day and a half during which he and alliance partners in the SACP and COSATU were effectively accused of being 'part of a dark conspiracy'. While Cronin was forced to make a public apology for betraying the confidentiality of NEC discussions, he insisted that he stood by the substantive points he had made.[24]

Many believe that the terms of the Hefer commission of investigation in 2003–4 were also adapted in a bid to embarrass the long-time Mbeki foe and former minister of transport, Mac Maharaj, who had alleged (without evidence) that the director of public prosecutions and a Mbeki loyalist, Bulelani Ngcuka, was an apartheid spy.[25] Mbeki was further criticised for being too thin-skinned in the face of media criticisms, and his relationship with the South African press deteriorated badly during his presidency. He used a weekly online column to attack several of his political opponents as well as the country's still racially untransformed media.

In 1998 Mbeki criticised the Truth and Reconciliation Commission's report for its condemnation of alleged ANC torture and execution of dissidents in its camps in Angola, which he saw as failing to distinguish between crimes committed by oppressors and those resisting oppression. He unsuccessfully sought a court injunction to prevent the report's publication. In 2004, Mbeki responded harshly to Archbishop Desmond Tutu's observations that South Africa was sitting on 'a powder keg of poverty'; that only a tiny elite benefited from the government's black economic empowerment (BEE) programme; and that sycophancy had replaced robust debate in the ANC. This elicited a harsh reply from Mbeki, who said: 'Those who present themselves as the greatest defenders of the poor should also demonstrate decent respect for the truth, rather than indecent resort to empty rhetoric.'[26] It should be noted that some of the public attacks against Mbeki by critics such as Xolela Mangcu and Justice Malala were of a personalised and emotional nature, and often lacked both subtlety and substance.[27] The blacklisting of certain anti-government critics by the state-funded South African Broadcasting Corporation (SABC) will remain a blemish on the Mbeki administration's record, even if this did not quite reach the depths of Kwame Nkrumah's press censorship in Ghana.

For their part, Mbeki's supporters argued that his 'imperial presidency' was no different from that of French presidents from Charles de Gaulle to Jacques Chirac or of British prime ministers like Margaret Thatcher and Tony Blair. Mbeki's public champions like Ronald Suresh Roberts and Christine Qunta sought to highlight the personal and ideological agendas of his critics, who they felt were uncomfortable with an assertive, intelligent pan-African leader who was not afraid to force whites to confront issues of race and poverty directly.[28]

Another criticism of Mbeki's administration was that not enough was done to root out corruption and incompetence. By far the most egregious and potentially damaging case was the controversial arms deal, concluded between 1997 and 1999 with firms from Britain, Italy, Germany and Sweden, that was worth R30 billion (about $4 billion) at the time, but that subsequently rose to R43 billion (about $6 billion). As deputy president, Mbeki was in charge of the arms procurement programme, and was subsequently accused by the Johannesburg *Sunday Times* of benefiting personally from this deal to the tune of R30 million, allegedly paid by a German ship-building company.[29] This allegation was denied by Mbeki through a spokesperson and was never substantiated. When *Business Day* accused Mbeki of seeking to doctor the report of the arms deal investigation which he had ordered, Thabo condemned these allegations as based on the racist belief that black governments would always be corrupt.[30]

Andrew Feinstein, the ANC chair of the parliamentary standing committee on public accounts, refused to adopt the committee's report on the arms deal in parliament, and eventually had to resign his parliamentary seat. Mbeki and his cabinet ministers later gave evidence to the Willie Seriti Commission on the arms deal in July 2014, with the former president failing to recall crucial details and noting that decisions of government in relation to the deal had been taken collectively.[31]

Mbeki also consistently defended his national commissioner of police, Jackie Selebi, whom he had appointed to office. When Vusi Pikoli, the director of the National Prosecuting Authority, tried to arrest the police commissioner, he was suspended by the president from office in September 2007 – according to Mbeki, because such a step would have resulted in a violent stand-off between different government agencies. Selebi was eventually sentenced to 15 years in prison in August 2010 for having accepted bribes from a drug baron, Glenn Agliotti, in exchange for passing on confidential police reports. In February 2008, a report by the Public Services Commission noted that cases of corruption within the civil service had doubled, and only 18 per cent of perpetrators were said to have been dismissed as a result of findings of graft.[32]

* * *

Already as deputy president, Mbeki, the philosopher-king and prophetic leader, began calling for an African Renaissance. This vision had antecedents in the thoughts and writings of Nigeria's Nnamdi Azikiwe, Senegal's Cheikh Anta Diop and Pixley Seme. Seme, one of the founding members of the ANC and its president-general between 1930 and 1936, gave a famous speech in 1906 at Columbia University, where he was the first black South African graduate, aptly entitled *The Regeneration of Africa*, which Kwame Nkrumah memorably quoted in its entirety at a Congress of Africanists in Accra in December 1962. Employing words that Mbeki would later use to title his most famous speech in 1996, Seme noted, 'I am an African', before lyrically setting out his vision of a regenerated continent: 'The brighter day is rising upon Africa. Already I seem to see her chains dissolved, her desert plains red with harvest, her Abyssinia and her Zululand the seats of science and religion, reflecting the glory of the rising sun from the spires of their churches and universities. Her Congo and her Gambia whitened with commerce, her crowded cities sending forth the hum of business, and all her sons employed in advancing the victories of peace – greater and more abiding than the spoils of war … The regeneration of Africa means that a new and unique civilisation is soon to be added to the world.'[33]

Mbeki's own vision of an African Renaissance was inspired by his shock at discovering what he regarded as the 'slave mentality' of black South Africans after his return home from exile in April 1990. As he put it, 'The beginning of our rebirth as a Continent must be our own rediscovery of our soul … It was very clear that something had happened in South African society, something that didn't happen in any other African society. The repeated observation is that "These South Africans are not quite African, they're European."'[34] Mbeki also criticised the black intelligentsia, many of whose members he felt were timid and too deferential to their white colleagues. He was determined, through his African Renaissance, to reverse damaging stereotypes about the continent, remarking in September 1995: 'Many in our society genuinely believe that as black people we have no capacity to govern successfully, much less manage a modern and sophisticated economy. These are very quick to repeat the nauseating refrain – look what has happened in the rest of Africa!'[35]

Mbeki also sought to use the Renaissance vision to persuade fellow South Africans to embrace not just a new South African identity, but a new African identity as well. As Mbeki said: 'No longer capable of being falsely defined as a European outpost in Africa, we are an African nation in the complex process simultaneously of formation and renewal … We will work to rediscover and claim the African heritage, for the benefit especially of our young generation.'[36] As Ali Mazrui noted, no African leader other than a black South African president could have made Mbeki's 'I am an African' speech without being marched off to an asylum. In the speech, Mbeki set out an inclusive definition of an African that represented a stirring attempt to encourage his compatriots to embrace and celebrate the African identity they had long been denied by white rulers. In this lyrical speech delivered on the occasion of the adoption of the South African Constitution, he told the Constituent Assembly:

'I am an African.

'I owe my being to the hills and the valleys, the mountains and the glades, the rivers, the deserts, the trees, the flowers, the seas and the ever-changing seasons that define the face of our native land …

'I am formed of the migrants who left Europe to find a new home on our native land. Whatever their actions, they remain part of me. In my veins courses the blood of the Malay slaves who came from the East …

'I am the grandchild of the warrior men and women that Hintsa and Sekhukhune led, the patriots that Cetshwayo and Mphephu took to battle, the soldiers Moshoeshoe and Ngungunyane taught never to dishonour the cause of freedom.'[37]

Though this particular speech was widely praised, Mbeki's views on race were often criticised. Some were unsettled by 'the prominence of race in Mbeki's worldview', which was puzzlingly labelled 'racial nationalism'.[38] Others depicted Mbeki as 'someone who essentialised race' and as a result hindered the process of building a common national identity. But, since the history of South

Africa had been founded on centuries of race-based dispossession of blacks as well as white 'affirmative action', and half a century of institutionalised racism, how could race not be a major preoccupation of a post-apartheid black leader? The attempt to stifle racial debates, in fact, remains one of the most dangerous time-bombs for the future of South Africa. This 'race denialism' is also one of the most disingenuous devices of a continuing albinocratic culture, occurring – until the 2015 'Rhodes Must Fall' and similar movements – even in South African universities, where such debates should have been flourishing.

Some have used apparently negative phrases like 'Africanist', 'Afrocentrism' and 'nativist' to describe Mbeki's views on race. Not only are these terms woolly and meaningless, but their use tends implicitly to contrast Mbeki's presumed European 'modernism' and sophistication with what often appeared to be a more 'primitive' Africanism.

In contrast, others have sought to explain rather than to condemn. Noting the pervasive view that most whites have expected a black government to fail, Steven Friedman, for instance, set Mbeki's concerns with race in the context of an overwhelming desire by a black government to persuade prejudiced whites of its competence in governing a complex, industrialised state. At the same time, Friedman criticised the black elite's obsession with demonstrating technical and managerial competence, for having led to a distorted set of priorities in which progress was measured not by how much the impoverished black majority's needs were being met, but by whether Western standards were being attained.[39] Alan Hirsch, chief director of economic policy at the Presidency under Mbeki's administration, confirmed the unwillingness of even a pan-African like Mbeki to look to African examples in social and economic policy, when he commented: 'The ANC's approach is sometimes summarized as elements of a northern European approach to social development combined with elements of Asian approaches to economic growth, within conservative macroeconomic parameters.'[40]

This was ironically the clearest sign of an inferiority complex, even as Mbeki was striving to prove the opposite. Friedman noted another paradox: an Mbeki administration that had always prided itself on technical management was widely seen in its final years, when electricity outages began to affect the country, as a source and example of mismanagement and poor 'service delivery'. Friedman further argued that a technocratic approach to governance had weakened the quality of South Africa's democracy, with the government unable to translate the preferences of its citizens (and voters) into concrete policy from which they could benefit. As he noted, the policy wonks in the presidency 'knew all the newest social and governance theories but were deluded into believing that what was happening in their heads was also happening in the country'.[41]

* * *

Whereas Kwame Nkrumah had famously urged Africans in the 1950s to seek first the political kingdom, Thabo Mbeki's approach after 1999 could perhaps be described as 'Seek ye first the *socio-economic* kingdom, and all other things would be added to it'. Post-apartheid South Africa had inherited a nearly bankrupt economy that had been badly affected by international trade sanctions in the 1980s and that had built up a $16.7 billion external debt. The Soviet Union, to which many ANC members looked as a model of social organisation and development, had crumbled by 1991, while social democratic models in Europe were suffering their own crises. On taking office as the first ANC-led government, Mbeki and Mandela regarded their main task as winning credibility with international capital and ensuring international investment in South Africa's economy.

At the same time Mbeki was fully aware of the urgent need for wealth redistribution and the reduction or elimination of the gross poverty and inequality that prevailed in South Africa. As deputy president in May 1998, Mbeki talked of South Africa as a country of 'two nations' in a hard-hitting speech to parliament: a white population of about 9 million with a living standard equivalent to that of Spain; and a black population of 35 million with a living standard comparable to that of Congo-Brazzaville. Mbeki borrowed the idea of the 'two nations' from the British prime minister Benjamin Disraeli, who saw British society in the age of high capital becoming polarised between rich and poor, thus creating 'nations within the nation'.[42] Post-apartheid South Africa still remained deeply unequal, and one of Mbeki's nagging fears while in office was that the anger and frustrations of the black majority would boil over at the slow pace of socio-economic transformation.[43] Between 2005 and 2008 alone, 26,513 incidents of protest were officially recorded. As he put it in the 'two nations' speech: 'we are faced with the danger of a mounting rage to which we must respond seriously. In a speech, again in this House, we quoted the African-American poet Langston Hughes, when he wrote, "what happens to a dream deferred?" His conclusion was that it explodes.'[44]

Mbeki consistently called for a 'national democratic revolution' in line with ANC thinking, which was in turn largely derived from the SACP. He was certainly running a state that was 'national' and 'democratic', but the socio-economic 'revolution' always seemed a distant pipe-dream. Mbeki was, in fact, among the chief architects of the controversial move away from the redistributive, state-led Reconstruction and Development Programme (RDP) – which formed the ANC's election manifesto in 1994 and which set out to prioritise jobs, welfare, housing, education and health – to a neo-liberal, market-led Growth, Employment and Redistribution (GEAR) policy in 1996. GEAR, unlike the RDP, did not have any redistributive targets, and was designed to reassure potential foreign investors, at a time when the rand was under threat in international money markets, that the ANC government would adhere to the prevailing economic orthodoxy.[45] As Alan Hirsch, one of Mbeki's economic advisers, noted: 'Economic conservatives and representatives of business frequently warned the ANC that it should "not kill the golden goose" in its efforts to rectify South Africa's inequalities, through higher taxes, for example.'[46]

Mbeki was determined to prove the government's competence in managing the economy and regarded the maintenance of the local white business community's confidence as well as that of foreign investors as critical to promoting the socio-economic transformation of the country. GEAR was premised on a deregulated private sector driving export-led growth and attracting foreign investment, and was enthusiastically supported by South Africa's influential big business sector. It sought to reduce state expenditure, liberalise financial controls, privatise 'non-essential' state enterprises, cut tariffs to open up the trade regime, provide tax incentives to attract new investment, and ensure wage restraint.[47] Taxes were cut by R72 billion (about $10 billion) between 1994 and 2004, even as unemployment reached an estimated 40 per cent (officially around 25 per cent) of the potential working population. GEAR promised to create 400,000 jobs a year and sustain an annual growth rate in the economy of 6 per cent. But the government did not come close to achieving any of these goals. The economy grew by only

0.6 per cent in 1998, and 1.2 per cent in 1999. By this time, the private sector's overall share of fixed investment had dropped to 68 per cent, while the expected flood of foreign investment failed to materialise, even as Algeria, Angola, Egypt, Nigeria, Tunisia and Zimbabwe attracted more investment from abroad than South Africa.[48]

The ANC government seemed to lack confidence in its economic management and spent much time placating the white business community, raising questions about whether the party was really in power or merely in office. Mbeki – whom critics like Patrick Bond accused of 'talking left and walking right'[49] – later confirmed this sense of disempowerment to his biographer, Mark Gevisser, at being forced to sign up to the 'Washington consensus' of deregulation and marketisation through GEAR.[50]

When GEAR was introduced, Nelson Mandela's popularity was skilfully deployed to counter leftist critics in the Congress of South African Trade Unions (COSATU) and the SACP, who, from this time on, condemned what they called Mbeki's '1996 class project'. The SACP called for the replacement of GEAR by a coherent industrial policy, while COSATU's general secretary, Zwelinzima Vavi, declared the plan 'unworkable and unwinnable', and the confederation as a whole rejected GEAR. Mbeki responded in kind, treating the leaders of his alliance partners, Vavi and Blade Nzimande of the SACP, with barely disguised disdain. Addressing the SACP in July 1998, he accused opponents of GEAR of 'fake revolutionary posturing …

charlatans, who promise everything is good, while we all know that these confidence tricksters are telling the masses a lie'.[51]

The implementation of GEAR was characteristic of Mbeki: a top-down, technocratic approach by an elite vanguard within a party led by policy intellectuals. Madiba would later admit: 'I confess even the ANC learnt of GEAR far too late – when it was almost complete.'[52] In its introduction and implementation, the ANC, its parliamentarians and its coalition partners were effectively by-passed and not consulted on one of the most radical policy shifts in the post-apartheid era. Even the ANC policy guru in the Presidency, Joel Netshitenzhe, conceded in 2004 that GEAR represented a 'structural adjustment policy, self-imposed'.[53]

* * *

In 2007 the Nigerian political economist Adebayo Adedeji called for South Africans to 'deconstruct' their colonially inherited political economy, and cautioned the country not to pursue the timid approach of other post-colonial African states that had failed to transform their colonial legacy. But GEAR was not abandoned. Instead, between 1996 and 2001, parts of a few state-owned enterprises, in particular Telkom and South African Airways (SAA), were privatised; the large South African companies Anglo American, South African Breweries, Billiton, Old Mutual, Liberty, Datatec and PQ Holdings were allowed to move their primary listing abroad; foreign exchange controls were removed; and agricultural subsidies eliminated. As the economist Sampie Terreblanche lamented: 'For the MEC [minerals energy complex] and the rest of the corporate sector the "great prize" was to be exonerated of the huge apartheid debt that had accumulated on their "accounts" as they exploited black labour relentlessly over a period of a hundred years.'[54] Mbeki had given the corporate sector absolution without a proper confession or contrition. He would also oppose efforts to bring class action suits in American courts in 2002–3 against US companies such as General Motors, Ford, IBM and Daimler for their exploitative role in propping up the apartheid state.

Mbeki's support for the controversial policy of letting large South African corporates relocate abroad was undertaken in a bid to open up his country's oligopolistic domestic market to black entrepreneurs and foreign investors. It was also felt that as a result these companies would secure more capital (raised from foreign sources) to invest in South Africa. But as Hein Marais noted about the relocation of seven of South Africa's largest companies abroad: 'The word "looting" comes to mind. Yet it occurred not in a broken-down system (as in Russia in the 1990s), but as part of a phased economic strategy, managed by a democratic government espousing an African Renaissance.'[55]

GEAR was meant to create macroeconomic stability.

But, while the national debt, deficits and inflation all went down, growth remained static. By 2000 economic growth was lower than it had been in 1996, while unemployment increased by a staggering one million people in six years (between 1994 and 2000) in such areas as the public sector, mining, manufacturing and agriculture.[56] The manufacturing sector suffered particularly from what some described as 'deindustrialisation', above all in the clothing, textile and footwear sectors, which were nearly decimated by trade and industry minister Trevor Manuel's tariff reductions of 1995.[57] Imports rose by 44 per cent between 2000 and 2005, even as exports declined by 12 per cent in the same period.[58]

Even the United States, in the midst of the Great Depression of the 1930s, took government action under President Franklin Roosevelt to correct socio-economic inequalities and rein in exploitative oligopolistic 'robber barons'. Post-apartheid South Africa's black majority had suffered centuries of Great Depressions, and more imagination was surely needed to redress the massive inequalities between white and black. What was required was an innovative socio-economic transformation programme – a South African New Deal – to reverse the continuing legacy of socio-economic injustices in one of the world's most unequal societies. Yet Mbeki – a trained economist and skilled politician – opted instead for a cautious, conservative 'trickle-down' approach. While one must recognise the domestic and external constraints and difficulties faced by the ANC government, it had clearly thrown in the towel too quickly without seeking to pressure the powerful business sector – which appeared willing to make sacrifices in the euphoria of the post-1994 transition and afflicted by the guilt of having colluded with the apartheid regime – to do more to help transform the country. As Colin Bundy remarked, 'The ANC hitched its wagon to South African capitalism; and ever since then the major conglomerates have ridden shotgun, guarding their interests.'[59]

GEAR was pure alchemy: a futile attempt to turn lead into gold through mysterious incantations from neo-liberal prophets. It became a dogmatic religion to which its adherents insisted there was no alternative. Mbeki appeared to be relying on the 'magic of the market' to distribute wealth to the country's black masses, and only belatedly – with the promotion of a 'developmental state' from 2005 onwards – realised that the market distributes its rewards unevenly, and that the government would have to play a greater role in driving socio-economic development. From 2004, there was more public intervention in the economy to promote infrastructure, upgrade public services and develop skills.[60] But by the time Mbeki left office in September 2008, the inequalities he had inherited from the apartheid state still remained glaring: the top 20 per cent of South Africans (about 10 million people) received nearly 75 per cent of the country's total income, while the poorest 50 per cent (about 25 million mostly black people) got only 7.8 per cent.[61] Moreover, the expected flood of foreign investment turned out to be a cruel mirage. King Canute-like, Mbeki sought, but ultimately failed, to roll back the waves of globalisation and their pernicious effects on South Africa's economy.[62]

Alan Hirsch admitted in 2015 that decisions made before and after 1994 had contributed to persistent poverty and inequality in South Africa, as well as to pedestrian economic growth. He described the compromises between white corporate business and the ANC as demonstrating 'short-termist defensiveness and a lack of imagination about South Africa's future'. Hirsch highlighted poor policies that had been implemented after 1994: excessively radical liberalisation of agricultural markets; poorly conceived education reforms; and badly designed privatisation of state-owned enterprises. He also noted what might have been done differently: wealth and land should have been more radically distributed; competition policy should have tackled oligopolistic structures and not just anticompetition behaviour; a more vigorous industrial policy should have been implemented; and more support should have been provided for small businesses.[63] An opportunity had been lost.

* * *

The one policy that Mbeki consistently pushed as part of his socio-economic legacy was black economic empowerment (BEE), in a bid to build a black entrepreneurial middle class. The man who had once written as a Marxist in 1978 that 'black capitalism has no redeeming features whatsoever',[64] now became one of its strongest promoters. As a party in government after 1994, the ANC set out consciously to create a black capitalist class which would be both productive and patriotic. BEE aimed to ensure that black businessmen acquired assets in large corporations, that black managers occupied corporate positions, that black entrepreneurs benefited from government contracts, and that wealth in general was transferred from white to black hands.

In 2001 the Black Economic Empowerment Commission (BEEC), chaired by Cyril Ramaphosa, recommended to Mbeki that BEE be accelerated and clear targets be set for transferring assets to black hands in the private and public sectors. The government accepted his recommendations and followed up with a raft of legislation. Although critics howled that employment and growth would be harmed, Mbeki had been impressed with Malaysia's transfer of assets under the government of Mahathir Mohamad from a Chinese capitalist class to a Malay ethnic majority while still maintaining economic growth. His own BEE policy would be modelled on the Malaysian example, though its implementation was eventually much less successful. A large part of the motivation of BEE was to prevent a social explosion (one of Mbeki's perennial fears) and to ensure political stability by building a black capitalist class that had a stake in the country's future.

Apart from the white business class, the policy drew criticism from the ANC's alliance partners, COSATU and the SACP, who were sceptical of this approach, and critical of BEE for creating a privileged group of black millionaires. They saw the policy as a form of 'elite empowerment' and 'crony capitalism' that benefited only a tiny elite of ANC-connected individuals, such as the 'big four' of Saki Macozoma, Cyril Ramaphosa, Tokyo Sexwale and Patrice Motsepe.[65] Defenders of BEE, however, pointed to the increase in the number of black and women managers. They also took issue with the obsessive focus on the equity element of BEE for simplistically depicting the initiative as handing out shares to influential black individuals, rather than focusing on the other aspects of BEE: management and control, employment equity, skills development, enterprise development, preferential procurement, and small enterprises.[66] In response to some of the criticisms, the Mbeki government embarked in 2003 on a belated attempt to extend BEE to make it more 'broad-based', with more projects devised to benefit local communities, rural populations and wider constituencies.

In addition to promoting the growth of a black middle class, the Mbeki government also continued the extension of services and facilities to the poor majority begun under Mandela, and massively expanded the provision of pensions and grants, especially from 2003 onwards. As a result, South Africa has today one of the world's largest programmes of social assistance, unequalled in terms of its expenditure and reach. Some criticised this welfarist approach as creating a 'culture of dependency', and called instead for the prioritisation of wealth creation. But the country enjoyed 14 consecutive years of economic growth between 1994 and 2008; the number of people benefiting from social welfare assistance increased from 2.5 million in 1995 to 12 million in 2007; the government built 2.3 million housing units between 1994 and 2008 (though the quality and durability of these houses have often been questioned); and expanded electricity provision to 80 per cent of households by 2007.[67]

Mbeki provided South Africa with macroeconomic stability and managed to promote socio-economic reforms more rapidly than any other post-colonial African state achieved.[68] But this neither created sufficient jobs, alleviated poverty quickly enough, nor created a large class of productive and socially conscious black entrepreneurs. Groups such as the Landless People's Movement and the Anti-Privatisation Forum sprang up to challenge the exclusion of the poor and marginalised from society and to oppose the government's conservative economic policies. Power-cuts and load-shedding, which occurred across South Africa in 2007, further exposed some of the incompetence within the Mbeki administration, since the government had been warned a decade earlier to build new power stations. Mbeki would uncharacteristically apologise to the nation for this failing in December 2007.

* * *

Two other key areas for the social and economic advancement of the black majority that had been historically neglected by colonial and apartheid governments were education and health. But they continued to suffer from debilitating inequalities during Mbeki's leadership. After 1994, an apartheid system persisted in the educational sphere: in 2009, 11,000 of the 17,000 students in the country's 100 best performing schools were still white. In stark contrast, a South African education department survey of grade six learners (age 12) found that only 19 per cent were proficient in maths and just 37 per cent in reading and writing at their level.

Some of the blame for this poor performance was put on the outcomes-based education (OBE) approach to learning, which was borrowed from old 'white dominion' countries like Australia, Canada and New Zealand. South Africa eventually abandoned OBE in 2009.[69] With Zimbabwe having trained many thousands of able teaching professionals after independence, it was surprising that Mbeki – the prophet of Africa's Renaissance – did not look across the Limpopo to see what lessons he could learn from his neighbour.

Despite South Africa spending 8.7 per cent of GDP on health by 2008, the system remained an apartheid one. About 60 per cent of money spent on health went to funding private health-care for a largely white population of 7 million people. The public sector, to which the majority of (mostly black) people turned, suffered from maladministration, lack of basic facilities, and gross inefficiencies.[70]

Undoubtedly, the most controversial policy of Thabo Mbeki's presidency was what his critics dubbed his 'AIDS denialism'.[71] South Africa was estimated to have the largest number of people infected with HIV/AIDS in the world, at over 5 million by 2008, but its president said in 2003 that he did not know anyone who had died of the disease. Mbeki set up a presidential AIDS advisory council, half of whose members belonged to the 'dissident camp' of scientists who did not believe in mainstream views that HIV necessarily caused AIDS. Though Mbeki denied holding this view himself, his advisory panel and he himself sent out mixed messages on this issue, which many felt negatively affected public information campaigns on HIV/AIDS.

An earlier incident that had damaged Mbeki's credibility on this issue involved his support, as deputy president, and that of the health minister, Nkosazana Dlamini-Zuma, for Virodene, a drug produced by scientists at the University of Pretoria from a toxic industrial solvent, which turned out to have no antiretroviral effects. Mbeki and Dlamini-Zuma allowed the cabinet to be briefed by the scientists on preliminary findings that had been neither controlled nor peer-reviewed.[72] When the Medicines Control Council put a stop to the clinical trials of the drug as being unethical and unsafe, its chair, Peter Folb, was dismissed.[73] Though one can understand that a government with the worst HIV/AIDS infection rates in the world would be desperate to find a home-grown solution to the pandemic, this was clearly a lapse of judgement. Dlamini-Zuma later led parliament to pass the Medicines and Related Substances Control Amendment – for the production of generic antiretroviral (ARV) drugs – which came into effect in 1997.

The ANC government did not, however, take im-mediate advantage of the Act, announcing by March 1999 that it would not sanction the use of AZT due to its high costs and alleged toxicity.[74] These arguments were largely credited to Mbeki. By this time, an estimated 30,000 lives could reportedly have been saved with the provision of these drugs to pregnant women.[75] Dlamini-Zuma acted courageously in informing Mbeki directly of the damage that his public musings on AIDS were having on South Africa's international reputation, prompting the president to withdraw from the debate.[76] Underlining the fear instilled by Mbeki's rule, it had taken two full years for a senior ANC politician to criticise the leader's damaging stance on HIV/AIDS.

Kader Asmal recalls a tempestuous cabinet meeting in 2003 on the roll-out of antiretrovirals at which Mbeki and his health minister, Manto Tshabalala-Msimang, argued strongly against the distribution of ARVs.[77] Mbeki finally agreed to roll out ARVs in earnest in 2004 after the Constitutional Court had ordered his government to do so two years earlier. The Mbeki administration also came under pressure from the medical community, civil society groups such as the Treatment Action Campaign (TAC), trade unions and churches, as well as prominent figures like Nelson Mandela and Desmond Tutu. Another decisive intervention was made by Mbeki's international investment council (which included figures like George Soros and Niall FitzGerald), which cautioned Mbeki about the negative effect that South Africa's AIDS policies were having on foreign investment.

The explanations offered for Mbeki's obstinate stance on this issue revolve around his strong rejection of claims that AIDS originated in Africa and that it was spread by what was sometimes stereotypically depicted as un-controlled black sexuality.[78] A Harvard University study published in November 2008 estimated that 365,000 people could have avoided premature death if ARVs had been provided timeously. Regardless of his reasons for this stance, it is clear that the AIDS debacle will do the most damage to Mbeki's presidential legacy. In historical terms, this will be the worst blemish on his record.

* * *

Mbeki won a second presidential term in 2004 with a campaign in which he personally loosened up on the trail, famously sitting once on the floor in a township shack. The ANC won 69 per cent of the votes, though participation in the polls by the voter-age population had declined from 86 per cent in 1994 to 57.8 per cent in 2004. Despite the victory, a political crisis would soon unfold that would have a devastating impact on Mbeki's presidency and ultimately lead to his downfall. Following corruption allegations, Thabo sacked his deputy president, Jacob Zuma, in a parliamentary speech in June 2005 during which his hands were visibly trembling. Thereafter, Mbeki's popularity steadily eroded and the party (which still insisted on retaining Zuma as its deputy president) became deeply divided.

The relationship between the two men had already cooled four years earlier when Mbeki reportedly accused Zuma of passing on confidential information to alleged anti-Mbeki plotters Cyril Ramaphosa, Mathews Phosa and Tokyo Sexwale.[79] With Zuma managing to avoid conviction for both corruption and rape charges a year later, Mbeki looked increasingly isolated. Many critics saw opposition to what they regarded as Mbeki's autocratic leadership style, rather than pro-Zuma enthusiasm *per se*, as having accounted for Zuma's political ascendancy. As Mzukisi Qobo elegantly noted: 'Like the central character in Mary Shelley's novel, *Frankenstein*, who was deeply cynical about humanity and turned loose upon society a monster that would wreak unstoppable havoc, Mbeki fomented the climate that allowed Zuma to wrestle back power. Zuma is Mbeki's political engineering gone wrong.'[80]

By 2007, the ANC was split, with loyalists of both camps using intelligence agencies against each other: for example, Ronnie Kasrils, Mbeki's loyal minister of intelligence, fired his director-general and Zuma ally, Billy Masetlha, for alleged spying on ANC members.[81] Ethnicity was also increasingly mobilised in a ferocious battle: Mbeki was accused of relying on a 'Xhosa Nostra' – members of his ethnic group – who were overrepresented in his cabinet.[82] At the party's Polokwane conference in December 2007, Mbeki lost the party presidency to Jacob Zuma by a margin of 60 per cent to 40 per cent. In the aftermath, divisions deepened within the ANC and there were troubling threats to 'Kill for Zuma'. Polokwane had seen the mobilisation behind Zuma of a 'coalition of the wounded': COSATU, the SACP and the ANC Youth League. Ben Turok vividly described the mood he observed in Polokwane: 'People said they were fed up with [Mbeki's] arrogance, his intolerance of dissent, and the failures of service delivery.'[83]

Following Mbeki's ousting from the presidency in September 2008, a splinter party appeared within two months, calling itself the Congress of the People (COPE). It was led by the senior ANC figures Sam Shilowa and Mosiuoa Lekota. COPE would itself soon become damaged by factionalism, and failed to provide a credible alternative to the ANC. South Africa's potent mix of populism, violence, poverty and political instability raised serious questions about the state that Mbeki was leaving behind to his successors, as well as about his own ultimate legacy. As Andile Mngxitama observed in 2009, 'The populism of Zuma emerged as a direct consequence of the failure of Mbeki's market populism to address the issues of poverty, land, housing and health care. The spinning stats and Irish poetry couldn't hide the ugly truth.'[84]

* * *

When Judge Chris Nicholson cleared Jacob Zuma of corruption charges in September 2008 and implied that Mbeki had been part of an anti-Zuma conspiracy (a judgment that was overturned four months later on appeal), members of the ANC's National Executive Committee – led by the three men that Mbeki had accused of a plot in 2001, Cyril Ramaphosa, Mathews Phosa and Tokyo Sexwale – used this decision to 'recall' Thabo Mbeki from power, ending his presidency in the most dramatic of circumstances.[85] The ANC veteran Ben Turok offered a scathing epitaph on Mbeki's rule: 'he left behind levels of factionalism and corruption that the movement has not yet succeeded in containing. The historical irony is inescapable. Mbeki was determined to set the ANC and government on a new course; but it was under his leadership that the movement lost its direction.'[86]

In 2006 Achille Mbembe linked Jacob Zuma's followers to a millenarian form of politics, contrasting this vividly with Mbeki's modernism: 'There must emerge a false *maprofeti* (prophet), generally a person of very humble origins. Backed by a certain level of mass hysteria, the *maprofeti* then claims that a great resurrection is about to take place. Whenever questioned about the sources of his actions and authority, he invariably refers to the authority of his "ancestors", his "tradition" or his "culture" ... Although of a secular nature, the new millenarianism and nativist revivalism is using eschatological language of the "revolution second coming" in order to paint as the epitome of the Antichrist one of the most worldly, cosmopolitan and urbane political leaders modern Africa has ever known.'[87]

The story of Mbeki and Zuma also recalled the 1963 play by the Nigerian Nobel laureate, Wole Soyinka, *The Lion and the Jewel.*[88] Set in a pre-independence Nigerian village of Ilujinle, the story centres on the courting of a beautiful young woman, Sidi, by two men: Lakunle – a Westernised school teacher with little understanding of his own country and its customs – and Baroka, a traditional chief who resists modernisation and Western influences on his village. Both desire Sidi, but in the end it is the wily Baroka who wins the affection of the young woman by setting a devious trap in which he feigns sexual impotence in order to lure the 'jewel of Ilujinle' into the 'lion's den'. Baroka consummates the courtship, and Sidi agrees to marry him.

I watched a performance of the play in South Africa

in April 2008 as the power struggle between Mbeki and Zuma raged. Soyinka's play can, in a sense, be read as a parable of this political battle, with Mbeki representing the Westernised, urbane Lakunle who is out of touch with his own citizens; Zuma (who often wears Zulu traditional dress and is married to four wives) represents Baroka; while Sidi, the jewel, is the ANC presidency for which both men fought such a bitter struggle. In the end, it was Zuma who won both the jewel and the crown. Like Baroka, Zuma relied on guile and a better understanding of popular politics to mobilise support for his spectacular victory at the ANC's Polokwane conference in December 2007. Mbeki would finally meet his come-uppance in September 2008 when his party forced him to resign as the country's president. The prophet of Africa's Renaissance had suffered the same fate as his Shakespearian hero, Corolianus, in what can be seen as an epic African tragedy.

The foreign policy president

It is the area of foreign policy – particularly in Africa – that is likely to be the most noteworthy legacy of Thabo Mbeki's presidency.[1] Under his direction, South Africa established solid credentials for becoming Africa's leading power. As the 'Pied Piper of Pretoria', Mbeki piped the diplomatic tunes to which warlords, rebels and politicians danced as he led peace efforts in the Democratic Republic of the Congo (DRC), Zimbabwe and Côte d'Ivoire. In strategic partnership with Nigeria, he was instrumental in building the institutions of the African Union (AU), the New Partnership for Africa's Development (NEPAD), the African Peer Review Mechanism (APRM), the Pan-African Parliament, as well as increasing Africa's leverage in institutions of global governance such as the United Nations (UN), the World Trade Organisation (WTO), the World Bank and the International Monetary Fund (IMF).

During his administration, foreign policy was made at the Presidency by a man who had been secretary for international relations of the ANC and its long-time contact person with the outside world. His foreign minister throughout his administration was Nkosazana Dlamini-Zuma, though Mbeki relied heavily on his student friend and confidant, Aziz Pahad, as deputy minister.

At a foreign policy retreat in February 2001, Mbeki identified five key priorities for South Africa's external relations: restructuring the OAU/AU and the Southern African Development Community (SADC); reforming regional and international organisations such as the UN, the WTO, the World Bank and the IMF; hosting major international conferences; promoting peace and security in Africa and the Middle East; and fostering ties with the G-8, while devising a global South strategy.[2]

Mbeki was the first chair of the AU at its birth in Durban in 2002; he was chair of the Non-Aligned Movement between 1999 and 2003; and he was the intellectual architect of NEPAD. South Africa held the presidency of the influential Group of 77 (G-77) developing countries at the UN during critical debates on reforming the organisation in 2005–6, while the country won a two-year seat on the UN Security Council in 2007–8. Under Mbeki's leadership, South Africa hosted two high-profile UN conferences on racism and sustainable development. Mbeki further used 'sports diplomacy' to promote South Africa as an African power. The country hosted the Africa

Cup of Nations in 1996; helped to finance Mali's hosting of the event in 1998; laid the foundation for the hosting in South Africa of the first-ever football World Cup on African soil in 2010; and hosted the All-Africa Games in 2003. Mbeki also promoted 'cultural diplomacy' by financing the restoration of Mali's famous library in Timbuktu.

Mbeki's foreign policy was in part driven by his vision of an African Renaissance, which, as well as encouraging South Africans to embrace an African identity, sought to promote the continent's political, economic and social renewal, and the reintegration of Africa into the global economy. He urged Africans to adapt democracy to fit their own specific conditions without compromising its principles of representation and accountability. He further challenged them to discover a sense of their own self-confidence after centuries of slavery and colonialism, which had systematically denigrated their cultures and subjugated their institutions to alien rule. The African Renaissance did not naively assume, as some critics asserted, that this renewal was already under way: it merely sought to set out an inspiring vision and lay down the policy actions that could create the conditions for Africa's rebirth. Mbeki's African Renaissance had as its central goal the right of African people to determine their own future. It called for a cancellation of Africa's foreign debt, an improvement in Africa's terms of trade, the expansion of development assistance, and better access to foreign markets for African goods. Mbeki also pragmatically urged African governments to embrace the positive aspects of globalisation by attracting capital and investment with which to develop their economies.

As an insightful analysis by Peter Vale and Sipho Maseko has also commented: 'South Africa's idea of an African Renaissance is abstruse, puzzling, even perhaps mysterious, more promise than policy.'[3] With Mbeki as chief architect, the drafting of NEPAD in 2001 and the birth of the AU in 2002 were clearly attempts to add policy flesh to the skeletal bones of his Renaissance vision. There was certainly some truth to the criticism that the Renaissance was devoid of substantive policy content. Seventeen African Renaissance festivals were held each May between 1999 and 2015 in different South African cities, at some of which Mbeki delivered keynote addresses. But they mostly involved South African government, business, civil society leaders and musicians, and thus tended to be parochially focused on South Africa rather than the broader continent and its diaspora.

It remains a mystery why Mbeki did not use his ministers and other senior officials more effectively to promote the African Renaissance and to seek to build grassroots support for the concept within South Africa and across the continent and its diaspora. A rare example was the elegant speech of Mbeki's arts and culture minister, Pallo Jordan, 'Thoughts on an African Renaissance', delivered at the Aardklop festival in Potchefstroom in September 2005. Despite talk of an African Renaissance, South Africa's cultural schizophrenia was evident in the fact that its new rulers continued to refer only to its black population as 'African', leaving one wondering whether 'coloureds', Asians and whites were not also African. Furthermore, many black South Africans still talked about the rest of Africa as if they were not part of it. The fact that so many symbols of apartheid still littered South Africa's political landscape under Mbeki's rule astounded many African visitors.[4] Most astonishingly, outside South Africa's parliament – the deliberative body of Africa's greatest hope – stood a statue of Louis Botha, a white military conqueror and prime minister, on horseback. Nothing could better symbolise South Africa's cultural limbo, caught between a shameful past of arrogant European racism and a future, at which it was struggling to arrive, as the midwife of Africa's Renaissance.

* * *

Many African governments and people also expressed unease about what they perceived to be South Africa's xenophobic immigration and mercantilist trade policies under Mbeki's rule. They accused its leaders of ingratitude after three decades of continental support for the ANC at enormous cost to their countries. Senior South African Home Affairs officials called for a declaration of 'war' on 'illegal immigration', which they described as one of the country's 'major social and economic plagues'. In 2000 'Operation Crackdown' continued apartheid-era practices with the arrest of undocumented immigrants. People were also sent to the notorious Lindela detention centre, and Human Rights Watch reported that some undocumented migrants had died in detention. An estimated 177,000 Zimbabweans were deported between 2005 and 2006.[5]

Of even greater concern were the incidents of xenophobic violence. In 2006, 31 Somalis, many of them shopkeepers outcompeting locals, were murdered in Cape Town. Then in May and June 2008 there were horrific xenophobic attacks by rampaging South African mobs against foreigners from other African countries (mostly Mozambique and Zimbabwe), suggesting that the self-styled 'rainbow nation of God' was 'no longer at ease'. Sixty-two people were killed and about 100,000 displaced by this violence. There was much poignant symbolism in this situation. The embarrassment caused by the images beamed across the world was felt throughout the continent. In a sense, the xenophobic attacks represented the smouldering ashes of Mbeki's African Renaissance project.

Many Africans further complained about the aggressive drive by South Africa's mostly white-dominated corporations in search of new markets north of the Limpopo. South African business interests did not help their cause in Africa by talking as if they were determined to follow in the footsteps of Cecil Rhodes. The head of Standard Bank referred to a 'sense of pioneering'; the MD of Shoprite Checkers spoke of 'an army on the move';[6] while others talked of conquest.

During Mbeki's rule, South African firms established interests in mining, banking, retail, communications, arms and insurance, often with the active support of host governments. By 2003 South African companies ran Cameroon's national railroad and Tanzania's national electricity company, and managed the airports of seven African countries. In the same period, Shoprite's 72 shops in the rest of Africa sourced South African products worth R129 million rather than buying some of them – including basic items like eggs – in their host countries.[7] Local resentment swelled in places like Kenya, Tanzania and Nigeria at what some saw as mercantilist efforts to export apartheid labour practices and destroy homegrown infant industries. These criticisms should be balanced against the creation of jobs and improvement in infrastructure and services in these countries. By 2000 South Africa had become the largest single foreign investor in the rest of Africa. A year later, its investment in the rest of the continent had increased by a staggering 300 per cent since 1996 to R26.8 billion, as the excess capital built up during the years of sanctions under apartheid found profitable havens on the continent. By 2002 the rest of Africa accounted for 16.74 per cent of

South African exports, while imports to South Africa from the rest of Africa amounted to an anaemic 3.62 per cent.[8]

One important but often underreported aspect of this trade was that migrants from the rest of Africa set up restaurants, spaza shops, fast-food outlets, barbershops, craft stalls and Internet cafés in many South African cities. Moreover, the tens of thousands of mostly southern Africans who bought goods in South Africa to resell in their home markets also contributed an estimated R20 billion annually to the local economy (an estimated 450,000 African shoppers travelled by road and 90,000 by air to Johannesburg in 2005 alone).[9] These figures certainly contradict the depiction of African migrants as parasitic leeches who were exploiting South Africa, and rendered the horrific xenophobic violence in 2008 even more tragic.

In reaction to these concerns, Mbeki consistently stressed that South Africa had 'no great power pretensions' on the continent.[10] In February 2000 he established a $30 million African Renaissance and International Co-operation Fund to promote democracy, development and security in Africa. The Mbeki administration further initiated efforts in 2005 to ensure that South African firms assisted broad-based African Economic Empowerment (AEE) through strategic partnerships that promoted economic development in African countries, though not much progress had been made on this issue a decade later. South Africa also established embassies in all 15 SADC countries as well as in 18 other African countries – more than in any other region of the world.[11]

Despite these reassurances, in the minds of many southern Africans there remained uncomfortable parallels between the foreign policy goals in Africa of apartheid and those of Mbeki. Apartheid leaders had striven to secure the white state, promote economic and technical links with their neighbours, and establish the country as a leading continental power.[12] Mbeki shared the latter two goals, but rather than securing the white state for apartheid, he sought to create a state that lifted South Africa's black majority out of poverty. In both cases, the principal goal was to pursue the national interest to benefit specific groups *within* South Africa.

* * *

One of the most important aspects of Mbeki's foreign policy was its pan-African outlook and diasporic reach. In 2000 Mbeki travelled to Bahia in Brazil to receive an honorary doctorate from the local state university in a region whose population was largely descended from African slaves. After reading from a poignant poem, 'The Slave Ship', by the Brazilian poet Castro Alves, he told his audience: 'Brazil cannot achieve its full identity unless it celebrates, also, its historical and cultural connection with Africa,' before calling for the development of more Afro-Brazilian scientists, economists and businesspeople.[13] Mbeki also promoted the African Renaissance at the University of Havana, Cuba, in March 2001, and visited the US several times, notably addressing an African-American audience at Martin Luther King's famous Ebenezer Baptist church in Atlanta in May 2000.

Mbeki further sought to play a role in the small Caribbean island of Haiti. In January 2004 he was the only African head of state to attend the bicentenary celebrations of the country's slave revolt against France, following which it had won its independence as the first black republic in the world. South Africa provided R10 million to support the event. At the commemoration in Port-au-Prince, Mbeki noted: 'Today we celebrate because from 1791 to 1803, our heroes, led by the revolutionary Toussaint L'Ouverture and others, dared to challenge those who have trampled on these sacred things that define our being as African and as human beings. Today, we are engaged in an historic struggle for the victory of the African Renaissance because we are inspired by, among others, the Haitian Revolution. We are engaged in a struggle for the regeneration of all Africans, in the Americas, the Caribbean, Africa and everywhere, because we want to ensure that the struggle of our people here in Haiti, in the Caribbean, in the Americas, Europe and Africa must never be in vain.'[14]

Mbeki would follow up this visit by working with the Jamaican prime minister, Percival Patterson, to provide support (mainly arms) to the Haitian president, Jean-Bertrand Aristide, who was facing an armed rebellion by March 2004. Aristide was eventually pressured to leave Haiti, reportedly by American and French diplomats, an exit that Mbeki compared with the US-instigated military coup that toppled the Chilean government of Salvador Allende in 1973.[15] Aristide and his family were then offered political asylum in a government villa in South Africa, where the deposed Haitian president worked as a research fellow at the University of South Africa until his return home in April 2011. Though the domestic opposition and others criticised Mbeki's attendance of Haiti's bicentennial celebrations and his military support for Aristide, they missed the broader historical significance of the leader of the last black republic to gain its independence paying tribute to the first.

But Mbeki could also be inconsistent in his championing of the African Renaissance. In July 2007 Nicolas Sarkozy, the newly elected president of France, gave a speech in the Senegalese capital of Dakar in which he remarked: 'One cannot blame everything on colonisation – the corruption, the dictators, the genocide, that is not colonisation.' He went on to admit that France might have made 'mistakes', but expressed continuing belief in its 'civilising mission' and claimed it 'did not exploit anybody'. Straining credulity, he added: 'Africans have never really entered history. They have never really launched themselves into the future ... There is no room either for human endeavour, nor for the idea of progress.' This speech was widely condemned across Africa and in some French intellectual circles. Mbeki, who had earlier been insulted during his mediation efforts in Côte d'Ivoire by Jacques Chirac, who complained that the South African leader did not understand 'the soul and psychology of West Africans', incredibly sent Sarkozy a bizarre letter, published in *Le Monde*, in which he stated: 'What you have said in Dakar, Mr President, has indicated to me that we are fortunate to count you as a citizen of Africa, as a partner in the long struggle for a true African Renaissance in the context of a European Renaissance.'[16] Achille Mbembe's eloquent riposte perhaps best captures the surprise of many in Africa: 'That two years before he exits power, Mbeki would tie his impeccable pan-Africanist credentials to Sarkozy is but the latest paradox in the political journey of a man who has thrived on contradictions'.[17]

* * *

As we have seen, Mbeki's strategic partnership with Nigeria was crucial in his efforts to fulfil his vision of an African Renaissance. Before his accession to the presidency, relations between South Africa and Nigeria had reached a nadir after the hanging by the Abacha regime of the environmental activist Ken Saro-Wiwa and eight of his fellow Ogoni campaigners, which took place during the Commonwealth summit in New Zealand in November 1995. Mandela, believing he had received personal assurances from Abacha of clemency for the 'Ogoni nine' and feeling deeply betrayed, condemned the killings and called for oil sanctions against Abacha's regime as well as for Nigeria's expulsion from the Commonwealth.

The decisive intervention that changed relations between the two countries was made by Mbeki, then still deputy president. Having served as head of the ANC office in Lagos in the late 1970s, Mbeki understood both the country and its main players, as well as Nigeria's importance to Africa and its political influence on the rest of the continent. Together with South Africa's high commissioner, George Nene, he devised a strategy to engage rather than confront the Nigerian regime. Mbeki embarked on diplomatic missions to Abuja;[18] pulled South Africa out of the Commonwealth Action Group on Nigeria, which had been set up shortly after Auckland; and refused to sanction Nigeria before the UN Commission on Human Rights.[19] The first Nigerian high commissioner to South Africa, Alhaji Shehu Malami, presented his credentials to Mandela in August 1996.

Mbeki provided a detailed justification of South Africa's policy to parliament in May 1996.[20] Arguing that the country did not have the leverage to dictate to Nigeria, Mbeki urged South Africa instead to encourage efforts to support Nigeria's transition to democratic rule. He warned South Africa not to overestimate its strength in a fit of arrogance, and noted the failure of the West to take any action. Instead, Mbeki argued that Mandela had been set up for failure by powerful Western countries which had made critical noises to assuage domestic public opinion while quietly continuing to do business with Abacha's autocratic regime. It is probably not an exaggeration to note that this single incident would shape Mbeki's future policy of 'quiet diplomacy' towards Zimbabwe. He was determined not to suffer the same fate over Zimbabwe that Mandela had fallen victim to over Nigeria.

In 1999 South Africa's Thabo Mbeki and Nigeria's General Olusegun Obasanjo assumed the presidencies of their countries. Both were very different personalities: one a pipe-smoking, Sussex-trained economist and intellectual; the other a career soldier and engineer. The two men had a close personal relationship dating back to Obasanjo's tenure as Nigeria's military head of state between 1976 and 1979, when Mbeki served as the ANC representative in Lagos. Obasanjo had visited apartheid South Africa as co-chair of the Commonwealth Eminent Persons Group in 1986, in an attempt to promote negotiations between the ANC and the apartheid government. The Nigerian leader's first foreign trip abroad on becoming president was to attend Mbeki's inauguration in June 1999.

Mbeki and Obasanjo were both respected internationally, but faced enormous economic and political difficulties at home. The two leaders attempted to promote norms of democratic governance through the AU, whose founding charter they were instrumental in shaping. Prior to this, both had challenged the inflexible adherence of the AU's predecessor, the OAU, to absolute sovereignty and non-interference in the internal affairs of member states.[21] At the OAU summit in Algiers in 1999 they were successful in pushing for the ostracisation of regimes that engaged in unconstitutional changes of government. The organisation subsequently barred the military regimes of Côte d'Ivoire and Comoros from attending its next summit in Lomé, Togo. The two leaders also persuaded their colleagues that the OAU must recognise the right of other states to intervene in the internal affairs of its members in egregious cases of gross human rights abuses and to stem regional instability. These ideas were then enshrined in the AU's Constitutive Act of 2000.

Both Mbeki and Obasanjo further stressed the importance of conflict resolution in Africa. With the help of Mandela and later of his deputy president, Jacob Zuma, Mbeki lent his country's weight and resources to peace efforts in Burundi between 1999 and 2004. He was particularly critical of the military regime of General Robert Guei in Côte d'Ivoire and Revolutionary United Front rebels in Sierra Leone. As the AU mediator to the country between 2004 and 2006, he was active in negotiations to restore constitutional rule to Côte d'Ivoire, and helped persuade Liberia's Charles Taylor to leave power for exile in Nigeria in August 2003. Obasanjo similarly led peacemaking efforts in Liberia, Sierra Leone and the Great Lakes region. But both Nigeria and South Africa eventually felt the strain of peacekeeping burdens in Burundi (under the AU) and Liberia (under ECOWAS, the Economic Community of West African States) on their economies. South African and Nigerian peacekeepers increasingly served mainly under the UN, in line with their leaders' insistence that the world body take over these responsibilities from weak regional organisations. This not only represented an attempt to legitimise such military actions, but was also a conscious effort to alleviate local fears of aggressive regional hegemons pursuing their own parochial interests under the guise of peacekeeping in Africa.

Both Mbeki and Obasanjo further lobbied the rich world on behalf of Africa at annual Group of Eight meetings, though the results were often disappointing, as the G-8 did not deliver on its funding pledges to Africa. Both drove the NEPAD process, which Mbeki had largely devised. This was based on a straightforward bargain between Africa and its largely Western donors: in exchange for support from external actors, African leaders agreed to take responsibility for, and commit themselves to, democratic governance. In October 2001, 16 African leaders met in Abuja for NEPAD's first implementation meeting.[22] As key members of NEPAD's implementing committee, Mbeki and Obasanjo pushed 26 of their fellow leaders to sign up to its peer review mechanism, though critics argued it lacked the 'teeth' to deal with autocratic offenders. Many African civil society organisations also dismissed NEPAD as a conservative socio-economic plan that represented a 'top-down' imposition by leaders without much consultation with their citizens.

South Africa's efforts at promoting democracy and human rights have sometimes been met with fierce opposition from other African countries. After some difficulties with South Africa's peacemaking role in the DRC, Angola and Nigeria, Mbeki was forced to be more cautious when dealing with his closest neighbours and counterparts. SADC leaders like Zimbabwe's Robert Mugabe, Namibia's Sam Nujoma and Angola's Eduardo dos Santos felt that they had preceded Mbeki in the liberation struggle, and complained that the ANC-led government had not repaid the sacrifices their countries had made to the liberation of South Africa. In his efforts to break the political impasse in Zimbabwe, Mbeki worked closely with the leaders of Nigeria, as well as those of Malawi, Mozambique and Namibia.

Despite the domestic constraints on South Africa and Nigeria, the Tshwane–Abuja axis sought to drive the African Renaissance forward. As Obasanjo noted during a state banquet in Abuja in honour of Mbeki in 2000: 'Our location, our destiny and the contemporary forces of globalisation have thrust upon us the burden of turning around the fortunes of our continent. We must not and cannot shy away from this responsibility.'[23] In October 1999 both leaders established the South Africa-Nigeria Binational Commission (BNC), thereby formalising the strong ties between their countries. The commission outlined five objectives: to provide a framework for joint efforts to bring Africa into the mainstream of global political, social and economic developments; to provide the basis for the governments and private sectors of both countries to consult with each other to promote bilateral trade and industry; to improve bilateral relations in the fields of technology, education, health, culture, youth and sports; to use both countries' human and natural resources to maximise socio-economic development through collaborative efforts; and to establish the mechanisms to promote peace, stability and socio-economic integration in Africa.[24]

Six annual meetings were held, alternating between Nigeria and South Africa, between October 1999 and September 2004. Trade and investment formed one major topic: the 2002 meeting, for instance, initiated the idea of a free trade area involving both countries.[25] Foreign affairs was another. Both countries pledged to incorporate NEPAD into the work of SADC and ECOWAS; finalise plans to establish a 25,000-strong African Standby Force; urge other African states to join the African Peer Review Mechanism (APRM); and coordinate policies to strengthen Africa's position at the World Bank, the IMF and the WTO.

There were some strains in relations between Nigeria and South Africa that the BNC also sought to address. Nigerian diplomats often complained about negative press reports and xenophobic stereotypes of Nigerians as drug-traffickers and criminals in the South African media and popular imagination.[26] A Johannesburg radio station, Radio Highveld, was forced by the Broadcasting Complaints Commission to apologise after it claimed that Obasanjo was carrying cocaine in his bag when he came to attend Mbeki's inauguration in June 2004.[27]

Under Mbeki and Obasanjo, bilateral trade between the two countries increased greatly, with Nigeria becoming South Africa's largest trading partner in Africa, a relationship worth R17 billion by 2008. (This had increased to R45 billion by 2015.) After 1994, South Africa's corporate community began to view Africa's largest market with great interest, assisted by its long-serving and energetic high commissioner in Abuja, the former trade unionist Bangumzi Sifingo.[28] The South African telecommunications giants MTN and M-Net blazed the trail and listed on the Nigerian Stock Exchange. MTN spent $340 million launching its mobile telephone network in Nigeria in August 2001. By 2003/4, MTN Nigeria's post-tax profit of R2.36 billion had surpassed MTN South Africa's R2.24 billion profit. In June 2004, MTN had 1.65 million subscribers in Nigeria, which increased tenfold to 16.5 million by December 2007, representing a staggering 29 per cent of all its African subscribers in 16 countries, and more than its 14.8 million South African subscribers.[29] It was MTN's success that convinced many other South African firms that Nigeria was worth investing in.

Other prestigious companies that followed MTN into Nigeria included Stanbic, Rand Merchant Bank and Alexander Forbes. Within a year of operations, Stanbic's Nigerian affiliate was contributing 13 per cent of its Africa-wide revenues.[30] Sasol, the world's largest producer of petrol from coal, made a $1.2 billion investment in Nigeria to export natural gas. The government-funded Industrial Development Corporation (IDC) invested in Nigerian oil, gas, infrastructure, tourism and tele-communications. Spoornet worked with the Nigerian Railway Corporation to revive Nigeria's railways. Protea established hotels across the country.[31] Fast-food chains Chicken Licken and Debonairs Pizza set up franchises in Nigeria. Shoprite opened an outlet in Lagos in 2006, which became profitable within a year. Despite these successes, many Nigerians were resentful of the fact that the relationship seemed to favour South Africa disproportionately, arguing that the South African market remained closed to Nigerian companies and that over 90 per cent of its own exports to South Africa consisted of oil.

The alliance with Nigeria was a marriage of necessity

for Mbeki. Unable to assert leadership effectively in southern Africa because of residual historical problems, and facing rivalry from states like Angola and Zimbabwe that saw themselves as aspiring regional leaders, he almost seemed to be venturing outside his own subregion in search of viable allies and additional legitimacy to bolster his continental leadership ambitions. South Africa reached out to Africa's most populous state – Nigeria – and worked closely with it in diplomatic forums in pursuit of continental initiatives like NEPAD and the AU. This sometimes created tensions in the relationship with Nigeria: some of Obasanjo's professional diplomats and policy advisers privately criticised him for having too soft a spot for Mbeki and for ceding too much intellectual influence to Mbeki and his mandarins, who they felt were less experienced in the labyrinthine intricacies of African diplomacy than Nigeria's diplomats.[32] The fact that the relationship between both countries relied too heavily on the personal relationship between Mbeki and Obasanjo also created its own problems. There were many calls to institutionalise the bilateral relationship between Tshwane and Abuja, so that it would survive the exit of both leaders from the national stage. The establishment of a binational commission and growing commercial ties did not, however, overcome this problem. Relations between the two men's successors, Jacob Zuma and Goodluck Jonathan, were particularly frosty between 2010 and 2015, and during this time Angola seemed to become a more strategic partner for South Africa than Nigeria.

There were some tensions between the two countries over Zimbabwe during the Commonwealth summit in Abuja in December 2003. Mbeki had sought to ensure Robert Mugabe's invitation to the summit, while Obasanjo – under pressure from Britain, Canada and Australia – did not want to disrupt the summit he was hosting with this divisive issue, and failed to issue an invitation. In Abuja, Mbeki clumsily tried to replace New Zealand's Don McKinnon with a former Sri Lankan foreign minister, Lakshman Kadirgamar, but lost by 40 votes to 11, with Nigeria voting against the South African proposal.[33] By 2005, more serious tensions erupted in bilateral relations over a reformed UN Security Council, Côte d'Ivoire, and the AU chair. Both countries had consistently expressed an interest in occupying one of two permanent African seats on an expanded UN Security Council. Though this proposal failed to find enough support within the UN General Assembly in September 2005 (with most AU leaders having unsuccessfully insisted on two permanent seats with veto power for Africa), the acrimonious contest saw some Nigerian officials privately questioning the authenticity of South Africa as a black African state, while the South Africans manoeuvred behind the scenes to undermine Nigeria.

Tensions were also evident in Côte d'Ivoire. Mbeki became the AU mediator in Côte d'Ivoire in November 2004, and was able to negotiate an accord a year later.

But the Ivorian parties continued to squabble over its implementation, resulting in a failure to hold elections by October 2005. After South Africa blamed Forces Nouvelles rebels for blocking peace efforts, they withdrew support from Mbeki's mediation, accusing him of bias towards the Ivorian president, Laurent Gbagbo. The rebels then urged the AU chair, Obasanjo, to find an alternative way of resolving the dispute.

At a meeting of the AU Peace and Security Council on the margins of the UN General Assembly in New York in September 2005, ECOWAS was tasked with overcoming this impasse: a clear shifting of the locus of peacemaking away from South Africa.[34] The Nigerians increasingly faulted Mbeki's role in Côte d'Ivoire for allegedly seeking to claim all the glory from any peacemaking success and failing to report back on his efforts to Obasanjo, the AU chair, who had appointed him.[35] Though Mbeki and Obasanjo jointly visited Côte d'Ivoire in November and December 2005, it was clear that a rift had opened between both men. With Senegal also increasingly critical of Mbeki's mediation, South Africa's president stepped down from his role in October 2006.

The final area of discord between Mbeki and Obasanjo occurred at the AU summit in Khartoum in January 2006, when Mbeki (supported by other African leaders) successfully opposed the suggestion that Obasanjo continue in the AU chair for a third consecutive term. As with his Nigerian presidential bid, Obasanjo was not offered a third term in the AU chair. The incident apparently led to his early departure from the meeting.[36] The fact that no BNC meetings took place between South Africa and Nigeria between 2005 and 2007 was another source of concern. The visit of the new Nigerian president, Umaru Yar'Adua, to South Africa to meet Mbeki in June 2008 – which followed the first meeting in three years of the SA-Nigeria Binational Commission – helped to revive, to some extent, the relationship between both countries. But it was the Mbeki–Obasanjo era that remained the 'golden age' of Africa's most strategic relationship.

* * *

A large part of Mbeki's foreign policy was directed at Zimbabwe. Here his policy of 'quiet diplomacy' was widely criticised by the Western media, several Western governments and many South African analysts. Commentators have tended to focus disproportionately on the Zimbabwean case to criticise Mbeki's foreign policy. While one can rightly condemn the autocracy of Robert Mugabe, and while the deaths and human rights abuses in Zimbabwe are inexcusable, one wonders why there was not equal attention paid to the even more tragic cases of the DRC and Burundi in which Mbeki intervened, where over three million people have died since 1996.

In examining Mbeki's Zimbabwe policy, it is important to understand his past relations with Mugabe, which had been forged during the anti-apartheid struggle.

The ANC had supported the Zimbabwe African People's Union (ZAPU) rather than Mugabe's Zimbabwe African National Union – Patriotic Front (ZANU-PF). Fences thus had to be mended after Zimbabwe's independence in April 1980. Mbeki was instrumental in re-establishing relations with the new government in Harare, visiting the capital within three months of independence and meeting with senior ZANU-PF officials to establish an informal ANC presence in the country. Some of the conferences for the Planning for Post-Apartheid South Africa between 1987 and 1989 – centrally involving Mbeki – were also held in Harare.[37] These contacts helped establish a solid working relationship between Mbeki and Mugabe.

In the light of post-apartheid South Africa's difficulties in rallying regional support for initiatives in the DRC, Lesotho and Nigeria, and sensitive to accusations that South Africa was a 'Trojan horse' for promoting Western interests in Africa, Mbeki was careful not to become diplomatically isolated over the Zimbabwe issue. He thus refused to adopt the unilateral punitive actions advocated by many of his critics in the West (and South Africa) against the human rights violations of Mugabe's regime. Mbeki felt that his country had few alternative policies to deal with the Zimbabwe crisis, particularly since any spill-over effects from an implosion in its neighbouring country would bring even more refugees and some measure of instability to South Africa. (There were estimated to be over one million Zimbabweans living in South Africa, though no reliable count exists.) Mbeki therefore chose to 'contain' the situation through the controversial policy of 'quiet diplomacy', which sought – through discreet diplomatic contacts – to bring Zimbabwe's government and opposition together in an interim government. A violent election in March 2008 (in which Mugabe had lost the first round of the presidential polls to his opponent, Morgan Tsvangirai, requiring a run-off from which Tsvangirai withdrew) resulted in at least 200 lives lost. Mbeki's approach eventually yielded fruit in September 2008 with the signing of an agreement that created a government of national unity between Mugabe and Tsvangirai's Movement for Democratic Change (MDC), an accord concluded days before Mbeki himself was 'recalled' from power by the ANC.

Many of the analysts who focused solely on Mugabe's excesses seemed unable to grasp how important the land issue was to many black Zimbabweans. The country's liberation war had, after all, been primarily waged for land. But the remedies adopted by Mugabe, and the political expediency and economic damage involved in his 'fast-track' land reform initiative in 2000–3, proved greatly damaging for the country's economy.[38] Mbeki clearly recognised these problems in a leaked discussion document with Mugabe in August 2001. In it, the South African president acknowledged that while Zimbabweans should resolve their own problems, 'the party of revolution' – ZANU-PF – had allowed the economy to stagnate and living standards to suffer, thus alienating the masses as well as potential Western donors. African support for his administration was 'lukewarm and hesitant'. He thus urged ZANU-PF to 'rebuild its image as the servant of the people', and mobilise support among all important segments of society in which it had lost credibility.[39] As Mbeki bluntly put it to Mugabe, 'resort to anti-imperialist rhetoric will not solve the problems of Zimbabwe but may compound them.'[40]

After 1994, there were also trade tensions between Tshwane and Harare over South Africa's protectionist policies and use of its economic muscle in trade nego-tiations with Zimbabwe.[41] A proposed loan of $500 million from South Africa to Zimbabwe in 2005 reportedly included trade conditionalities obliging Harare to purchase agricultural inputs and petroleum from South Africa, as well as terms related to political and economic liberalisation.[42] This approach would seem to contradict widespread claims of Mbeki's naïve cosseting of Mugabe. What has also attracted little comment has been the fact that South African companies increased their market share in Zimbabwe's tourism, services and mining sectors, while industrial groups obtained bargains even in the midst of the country's socio-economic crisis.[43] Little noticed, too, was that, in order to promote its peacemaking goals in the Great Lakes region, South Africa needed Zimbabwe's assistance in resolving the DRC conflict.[44]

From 2000, Mbeki worked hard to have Britain, the United Nations Development Programme, the European Union, the World Bank, the IMF and the US help support a less chaotic land reform process in Zimbabwe. He often criticised Western governments for failing to fund these efforts. But by appearing to legitimise the flawed elections in 2002, by vociferously but unsuccessfully defending Zimbabwe from suspension from the Commonwealth in 2003, by opposing efforts by the UN Security Council to sanction Zimbabwe in 2007, and by adopting a distrustful approach towards Zimbabwe's opposition MDC – seen by some as backed by Western and white farming interests – Mbeki was widely criticised for appeasing an increasingly autocratic Mugabe.[45]

Interestingly, though Zambia and Botswana were critical of Mugabe, most SADC leaders pursued a similar line to South Africa's. It was Tanzania as chair of the SADC security organ that asked Mbeki to mediate in Zimbabwe in 2007, recognising its own lack of resources to sustain such a protracted process. Even after Mbeki left power in 2008, most SADC states continued to back Jacob Zuma's mediation efforts in Zimbabwe. After having left office, Mbeki rendered his own verdict on Zimbabwe's land reform efforts: 'the process of land reform in Zimbabwe has given land to at least 300– 400,000 new land owners, the peasants of Zimbabwe at last own the land. The programme succeeded and has this direct benefit on these huge numbers of Zimbabweans.'[46]

* * *

Given its size as one of Africa's largest countries, its strategic position at the heart of Africa, and its rich mineral resources, the Congo is the most important country for the stability of a large part of Africa: one of the key reasons why South Africa pushed for the country's inclusion in SADC in November 1997. During the early part of the Congo crisis from 1996, differences between South Africa and its interventionist neighbours – Zimbabwe, Angola and Namibia – paralysed SADC, and the OAU took over mediation efforts. South Africa, which had earlier supplied military materiel to Rwanda and Uganda, urged Kigali and Kampala to withdraw their troops from the DRC. An Inter-Congolese dialogue was held at the casino paradise of Sun City in South Africa in 2002 under Mbeki's leadership, and resulted in a power-sharing agreement between some of the country's key parties. South Africa also resolved to send 1,400 troops to a strengthened UN Mission in the Congo. Mbeki then brokered the Pretoria Accord between the DRC and Rwanda in July 2002, which led to the withdrawal of Rwandan troops from the DRC in exchange for a promise by the Congolese president, Joseph Kabila, to disarm anti-Kigali militias that had launched attacks into Rwanda from the DRC. A month after South Africa's diplomatic triumph, Angola brokered the Luanda

Accord between the DRC and Uganda, which resulted in the withdrawal of Ugandan troops from the Congo. In December 2002, Mbeki convened a meeting of Congolese parties in Pretoria to sign a transitional agreement, which laid down a two-year transition period during which Joseph Kabila would remain president of the DRC and run the country with four vice-presidents nominated from rebel groups and the unarmed opposition. The agreement also aimed at the reunification of the country, the adoption of a new constitution, the holding of national elections, the promotion of transitional justice and national reconciliation, and the disarming of armed groups.

Mbeki continued to be the main driving force behind the UN's verification mechanism for implementing the Pretoria agreement. In November 2003 he sustained diplomatic efforts by bringing the leaders of Congo and Rwanda to South Africa to discuss the implementation of their earlier accord. Mbeki eventually helped to steer the peace process towards the holding of the first multi-party elections in the Congo for 40 years, in July 2006, with South Africa's national electoral commission – under the leadership of Brigalia Bam – playing an important logistical and financial role.[47] It was important for South Africa to continue efforts to stabilise a country in which a two-decades-long war had claimed over three million lives, internally displaced over three million people, involved seven foreign armies, and spanned three of Africa's subregions. Building on Mbeki's peacemaking efforts, SADC members South Africa, Madagascar and Zambia contributed troops to the UN mission in the DRC. In 2013 a South African-led SADC force – also involving Tanzania and Malawi, and working under a UN umbrella – helped rout rebels in the volatile Kivu region.

A crucial part of South Africa's role in the DRC was economic: some even questioned the country's motives in playing such an active mediation role, wondering whether it was mainly because of its economic interests in the Congo.[48] These involved mining, agriculture, fisheries, energy, construction and communications. South Africa had already become the DRC's tenth largest trading partner by 2008, and South African companies operating in the country included AngloGold Ashanti, Anglo American, De Beers, Anglovaal, BHP Billiton, Kumba Resources and Mwana Africa. Some of these investments were large. For example, BHP Billiton signed an agreement to invest \$2.5 billion in an aluminium plant in Bas Congo in 2005. Some South African companies were also accused of using dubious means to pursue their business interests. For example, De Beers, Anglo American, Anglovaal and Iscor were all cited in a 2002 UN report on the illicit looting of the Congo's mineral resources.[49]

Under Mbeki's leadership, South Africa signed a bilateral agreement with Kinshasa in the areas of finance and infrastructure; and used government-linked organisations like the Industrial Development Corporation, the Council for Scientific and Industrial Research, and the South African Diamond Board to pursue its interests in the country. The most ambitious project in the DRC was Eskom's 15-year effort – begun under Mbeki – to transform the Congo's Grand Inga Dam into a source of electricity for much of sub-Saharan Africa. In a strategic move to gain subregional support, South Africa engaged the governments of the DRC, Angola, Botswana and Namibia to create a company, Westcorp, to fund the $5-billion third phase of the Inga project, which could eventually cost as much as $50 billion.

In neighbouring Burundi, Mbeki also involved South Africa in an important peacemaking and peacekeeping role. Nelson Mandela and Mbeki's deputy president, Jacob Zuma, had led peacemaking efforts among Burundi's parties from 1999. In order to ensure effective implementation of the Arusha Agreement of 2000, a cash-strapped AU mission in Burundi involving South African, Mozambican and Ethiopian peacekeepers was deployed to the tiny Central African country in February 2003.[50] The South African-led AU force helped stabilise the situation, before most of the AU troops were 're-hatted' as part of a broader UN peacekeeping force in May 2004.

* * *

Despite Mbeki's efforts at integrating South Africa into the rest of Africa between 1999 and 2008, it is unclear how this has been felt and acknowledged by South Africa's population and in particular its political and business elite. Many in Africa question whether Mbeki's successors in office will maintain the same level of commitment to the continent that he demonstrated during his eight years as president.

Some of the institutions that Mbeki built remain fledgling. The AU continues to suffer from a lack of capacity and funding; the African Peer Review Mechanism has been ineffectual in promoting democratic governance; while the Pan-African Parliament is a 'talking shop' devoid of substantive legislative powers. Assistance to NEPAD also failed to deliver the $64 billion a year that Mbeki and other African leaders had hoped for, leading to a widespread questioning of the initiative by African civil society groups, including even a founding NEPAD member, the Senegalese leader Abdoulaye Wade. The NEPAD secretariat in Midrand, South Africa, appears to have become a casualty of Mbeki's departure from power in 2008, as it struggles for funding, relevance and visibility.

The strategic alliance between South Africa and Nigeria was actively and skilfully promoted by Mbeki. Both countries must, however, pursue their leadership roles in Africa with sensitivity. In the debates about permanent seats for South Africa and Nigeria on the AU's 15-member Peace and Security Council, other states refused to accept any special permanent status or vetoes for either country, and instead created five three-year rotational seats to complement the ten biannual rotational ones.[51] South Africa and Nigeria will have to consult closely with other African governments and ensure that their actions are not seen as attempts to dominate the continent in pursuit of their own parochial interests. Only by taking measures to alleviate such concerns can South Africa and Nigeria become the beacons of democracy and engines of economic growth which Mbeki and Obasanjo clearly envisioned.

Despite its ignominious past, South Africa did, in a short decade and a half under Mbeki's leadership, transform itself from being Africa's most destabilising power under successive apartheid regimes to becoming its most energetic peacemaker. The country emerged as a credible African power and aspired to global middle-power status through building continental institutions and working through its African allies, as well as countries like Brazil and India in international political and trade forums where its voice was widely respected. In June 2003 Mbeki initiated the IBSA – India, Brazil and South Africa – dialogue forum, which built the foundation for the BRICS – Brazil, Russia, India, China, South Africa – grouping by 2011. This is the foreign policy legacy that Mbeki has bequeathed to his successors. As Ali Mazrui asserted, 'Thabo Mbeki has been more active [than Mandela] in Pan-African affairs from Haiti to Harlem, from Kingston to Kinshasa, from Togo to Timbuktu. South Africa under Thabo Mbeki is among the leaders of the re-globalisation of Pan-Africanism.'[52]

6

The post-presidency

Since Mbeki's fall from power in September 2008, his 'post-presidency' has been remarkably active.[1] He has been involved in peacemaking efforts in Zimbabwe, Sudan and Côte d'Ivoire; headed a UN panel to investigate illicit financial flows out of Africa; and sought to act as a public intellectual and critic in responding to major foreign policy – and, increasingly, domestic South African – issues. Earlier concerns that Mbeki might seek to 'rule from the grave' were, however, dissipated by the scale of his defeat as ANC president in December 2007 and the manner of his ousting from office nine months later.

Barely ten days before leaving office in September 2008, Mbeki had brokered an agreement to create a government of national unity in Zimbabwe. Its implementation would prove difficult amid wrangling over appointments to ministerial posts, provincial governorships and other senior positions. Though no longer president, Mbeki remained the SADC-appointed mediator in Zimbabwe. However, Morgan Tsvangirai, the MDC opposition leader, soon refused to continue to participate in peace talks unless Mbeki was removed as the mediator. Tsvangirai accused the deposed South African president of being pro-Mugabe and felt he had compromised his impartiality. Mbeki responded in kind, arguing that Tsvangirai was taking instructions from Western governments and that this had led to the failure to set in place a government of national unity.[2]

Mbeki eventually played an instrumental role in brokering an agreement in February 2009 by which Mugabe remained president, Tsvangirai was appointed prime minister, and ministerial and other posts were shared out between the government and opposition. In November 2009 Jacob Zuma appointed his own mediation team for Zimbabwe, and Mbeki left the position that he had occupied for two and a half years, having successfully shepherded a difficult transitional process and brought it to fruition. He would later condemn Western criticisms of the country's presidential elections in July 2013, which saw Robert Mugabe extend his 33-year rule, and also castigated the failure of Western governments to provide financial assistance for the country's land reform efforts, while strongly disapproving of the violence of land occupations. Mbeki further caused a stir when he revealed in November 2013 that former British prime minister Tony Blair had tried to pressure him to join a military 'regime change' intervention to topple Mugabe in the early 2000s, a charge that Blair denied.

In his post-presidency, Mbeki also became involved in peacemaking efforts in Sudan's volatile Darfur region, where over 300,000 people have died since 2003. The historical roots of Sudan's conflict lie in a struggle of five decades between an often brutal and domineering centre in Khartoum and the subordinate provinces, including Darfur and South Sudan. The independence of the South following a referendum in 2011 did not resolve these problems, and may in fact have hardened Khartoum's military resolve to keep other provinces from seceding in future.

A 20,000-strong combined African Union and United Nations mission was eventually deployed to Darfur between 2007 and 2010. In March 2009 an AU High-Level Panel on Darfur, led by Mbeki, was set up and issued its report seven months later. The panel did not pull its punches in describing the 'extreme violence and gross human rights abuses' that had taken place in Sudan. AU heads of state, though not the UN Security Council, endorsed Mbeki's report. The role of this panel was then extended to involve one of coordinating international diplomatic efforts in Sudan alongside the UN. This development understandably created tensions with senior UN officials, and some regarded it as a 'power grab'. Intriguingly, Mbeki – the prophet of Africa's Renaissance – used two British and Dutch political and legal advisers for this assignment on a complicated African case.

Though Mbeki enjoyed the confidence of Khartoum, many in Juba, capital of the secessionist state of South Sudan, distrusted him because of his perceived closeness to the Sudanese leader, Omar al-Bashir, whom the International Criminal Court (ICC) had indicted as a war criminal.[3] Mbeki, along with most other AU members, argued unsuccessfully that the UN Security Council suspend the ICC indictment for a year (as it had the power to do) in order to facilitate the process of peacemaking.

While Mbeki and the Nigerian special representative, Ibrahim Gambari, sought to persuade Khartoum to engage in talks with Darfuri rebel groups, military events on the ground bedevilled their diplomatic efforts, and the Sudanese government and assorted armed groups remained locked in hostilities. By 2010 an incredible 25 per cent of Darfur's population, or 2 million people, were still displaced and in need of international assistance.[4] Mbeki continued to visit the region, urging reconciliation between Khartoum and Juba once South Sudan became an independent state in July 2011. After civil war erupted in South Sudan in December 2013, Mbeki continued his efforts to reconcile Juba and Khartoum so as not to exacerbate the internal South Sudanese conflict, which was then the subject of mediation efforts by the regional Intergovernmental Authority on Development. By 2014

Mbeki was also pushing for an inclusive national dialogue within Sudan involving all political parties and civil society organisations. Back home, tensions revived between Mbeki and Zuma over Sudan when it was revealed in February 2011 that the South African government would no longer pay what it deemed the high costs (R20.5 million) of Mbeki's travel to the region, asking that the AU take over these expenses.

* * *

After Laurent Gbagbo refused to step down when he lost a presidential election to Alassane Ouattara in Côte d'Ivoire in November 2010, Mbeki was sent by the AU in December to meet the key actors in Abidjan and prepare a report on what should be done. As in the DRC, Mbeki pushed for a political compromise involving direct talks between Gbagbo and Ouattara mediated by AU and ECOWAS leaders, which the victorious Ouattara understandably declined. Mbeki later wrote an angry article in *Foreign Policy*, in which he argued that elections should never have been held in Côte d'Ivoire as conditions were not propitious in such a militarily and politically divided country; that they had been held at all was due to international pressure. He also questioned the right of the UN to declare the victor at the polls and believed the UN had compromised its neutrality by intervening on behalf of Ouattara. In his view, France had used its position on the UN Security

Council to determine the future of its former colony.[5]

UN secretary-general Ban Ki-moon's chef de cabinet, Vijay Nambiar, responded to Mbeki's comments in the same forum. He noted that the Ivorian parties had determined the pace and outcomes of the electoral process in accordance with the Pretoria Accord of 2005 – which Mbeki had overseen – as well as the 2007 Ouagadougou Agreement; that Gbagbo's presidential mandate had expired in 2005; and that ECOWAS and the AU had both backed the UN certification of the results.[6]

Mbeki was certainly correct to point to Gallic lobbying of the UN Security Council to support its neo-colonial interests in the West African country. He was also right to criticise the UN mission for failing to halt human rights abuses against civilians, while it focused instead on ensuring that Ouattara's presidential mandate was respected. However, most members of the international community – and the vast majority of African governments – felt that Gbagbo had lost the election to Ouattara fairly and squarely. What is more, elections in Côte d'Ivoire had already been postponed six times, and Gbagbo's democratic legitimacy had been increasingly open to question.

Mbeki continued his active post-presidency by agreeing to chair the UN Economic Commission for Africa's panel on illicit financial flows. The panel, which was set up in February 2012, reported that capital flight from the continent from 1970 to 2008 amounted to between $854 billion and $1.8 trillion. Mbeki argued that the $50 billion illicitly leaving Africa annually undermined the continent's development efforts, particularly as it received $25 billion in aid (half of this sum) annually. Nigeria accounted for 30.5 per cent of these outflows, Egypt 14.7 per cent and South Africa 11.4 per cent. As Mbeki put it, 'Africa is bleeding.'[7] About 60 per cent of the illicit flows were from large companies; criminal activity accounted for 30 per cent; while 10 per cent was due to government and individual corruption. The panel made concrete recommendations to deal with the problems that the continent faced in this regard.[8]

* * *

In his post-presidency, a visibly liberated Mbeki – unburdened by state power – transformed himself into a public intellectual – as opposed to a philosopher-king. He at first concentrated only on issues of foreign policy, assiduously avoiding domestic politics. He visited and spoke at universities, high schools, business forums and women's groups both within South Africa and across the continent. He also held dialogues with other African leaders – under the aegis of the Africa Leadership Forum – on ways to promote regional integration, democratic governance and socio-economic development on the continent. He was awarded an honorary doctorate by Addis Ababa University in July 2010 for his peacemaking efforts in Africa; he won the Daily Trust African of the Year award in 2012 for his similar efforts in Sudan; and he also received the Obafemi Awolowo Leadership Prize in Nigeria in March 2015.

In 2010 the Thabo Mbeki Foundation was established, with Mbeki as its patron. Its goals included promoting the African Renaissance; serving as intellectual home for a continental African Renaissance movement; becoming a premier African centre for dialogue, research and publication; and ensuring that African voices were heard and respected on African issues.[9] Linked to the foundation was the Thabo Mbeki African Leadership Institute – of which he was also the patron – set up at the University of South Africa with the twin goals of training African youth on the political, economic and social renewal of their continent, and creating new African thought leaders. Students have since attended courses at the institute from across the continent, including South Africa, Zimbabwe, Nigeria, Ghana, Ethiopia, the DRC and Cameroon.[10] Though both institutions play a positive and active role in promoting debates and in training young Africans, a grassroots African Renaissance movement seems a distant pipe-dream. The question also remains whether these two bodies can acquire sufficient resources and institutional presence to ensure their continuation after their patron's demise: a key challenge for all similar institutions across the continent. In addition to these two institutes, plans were announced for the establishment of the Thabo Mbeki presidential library and museum at the University of South Africa.

* * *

In his public speeches Mbeki covered a wide range of issues: the scourge of corruption and dictatorship in Africa; the alarming 'brain drain' that was robbing the continent of trained professionals; the need to strengthen African civil society; the stalled implementation of NEPAD; Western fears of China's growing economic presence in Africa; the European Union's heavy-handed imposition of unequal trade agreements on Africa; the increased deployment of US troops on the continent; the heroic deeds of young revolutionaries of the 'Afro-Arab Spring' of 2011 who had toppled autocracies in Tunisia and Egypt; NATO intervention in Libya in 2011 which, according to him, had used the 'lie' of Muammar Qaddafi's impending attacks on Benghazi to pursue 'regime change' rather than let Libyans decide their own fate; the continuing marginalisation of Africa in the global order; the need to achieve an African Renaissance; and the passing of anti-gay laws in Africa.

In September 2012, Mbeki raised eyebrows with a piece in *The Thinker* commemorating the tenth anniversary of the African Union in which he criticised the AU's failure to undertake a 'serious, systematic and strategic review' of its operations and regarded the 'embarrassing and debilitating' delay in electing an AU chair (until the appointment of the former South African foreign minister, Nkosazana Dlamini-Zuma, in July 2012) as part of a 'malaise that is poisoning the African body politic'. He bemoaned Africa's failure to exercise its right to self-determination, pointing to inadequate socio-economic and cultural development, human rights abuses, and an attitude of 'disrespect by various world powers'.

In the article, Mbeki further condemned Africa's post-independence 'liberation coalition' as having been dominated by an unprincipled, corrupt, rent-seeking class. He decried the AU's failure to achieve integration and unity, and noted that the collapse of the Soviet Union had led to the rise of powerful Western hegemons with an aggressive desire to 'transform all other countries into their neo-colonies'. Mbeki also took to task financial capital's increased grip on the world economy. He further condemned the failure of AU members to integrate their decisions into domestic laws; to respect democratic rules and avoid military coups; and to rely excessively on Western donors to fund their security efforts. He did, however, credit the AU with laying the foundation for high economic growth rates, for its role in monitoring elections, and in establishing bodies such as the Pan-African Parliament, the African Peer Review Mechanism (APRM), the African Court on Human and Peoples' Rights, and the AU Peace and Security Council.[11]

As Mbeki was one of the AU's founding fathers, his

attack came across as akin to infanticide. In addition, having ruled South Africa for six of the ten years in question, he should surely have to accept some of the responsibility for the failures he identified. Many of the rent-seeking leaders that Mbeki condemned were also allies with whom he had worked closely. The Western governments he now criticised as 'neo-colonial' were the same governments he went to meet at annual summits of the G-8 industrialised countries to seek their economic assistance and military support for Africa.

While the 15-member AU Peace and Security Council has brought much-needed energy and focus to conflict issues in Africa, some of the other institutional successes that Mbeki claimed for the AU were more open to question. The South African-based Pan-African Parliament has been a toothless talking shop. AU leaders can still routinely ignore the unenforceable judgments of the African Court on Human and Peoples' Rights. Although Mbeki noted the usefulness of the APRM, as president of South Africa he also did much damage to its credibility. When the APRM released a report on South Africa in 2007 critical of the slow pace of socio-economic transformation and growing inequalities, and cautioning about the need to address the danger of xenophobia, Mbeki's administration strongly objected, irresponsibly dismissing the xenophobic threat as 'simply not true'.[12] Less than a year later, 62 foreigners were killed and 100,000 people displaced in some of the most horrific xenophobic attacks in post-apartheid South Africa.

* * *

Though Mbeki sought to avoid becoming embroiled in domestic political issues, he did enter into some of these debates from 2011. In December that year, he responded strongly to deny as 'malicious' allegations by Judge William Heath – appointed by Zuma as head of the Special Investigating Unit – that Mbeki had instigated rape and corruption charges against Zuma. Mbeki also threatened legal action in April 2015 when Willie Hofmeyr, the deputy national director of the National Prosecuting Authority, accused him of using the NPA in his political battles within the ANC.

The former president further broke his earlier pledge and intervened in domestic South African politics in October 2012 during a speech at the University of Fort Hare in honour of his mentor Oliver Tambo. He declared that he was 'deeply troubled by a feeling of great unease that our beloved motherland is losing its sense of direction, and that we are allowing ourselves to progress towards a costly disaster of a protracted and endemic general crisis'. He went on to bemoan 'a dangerous and unacceptable situation of directionless and unguided national drift', and, in typical fashion, quoted from *Hamlet*: 'The time is out of joint.'[13]

These remarks followed the killing of 34 miners by the South African police at Marikana two months earlier.

In December 2013, during funeral rites for Nelson Mandela, Mbeki asked South Africans not to 'betray what he [Mandela] and others sacrificed'. This was said at a time when Jacob Zuma was facing widespread criticism for spending millions of government money in refurbishing his personal homestead in Nkandla.[14] In March 2014, Mbeki again spoke out against 'personal aggrandisement',[15] which some commentators saw as a veiled attack on Zuma. After the Zuma administration used heavy-handed security personnel to remove Economic Freedom Fighters (EFF) parliamentarians who were disrupting the presidential 'State of the Nation' address in February 2015, Mbeki remarked in public that the president should have answered the question when he would pay back the money for his home in Nkandla, in order to avoid the fracas. And in November 2015, Mbeki noted at the Nelson Mandela Metropolitan University in Port Elizabeth: 'If you are in a position of leadership, you are in a position of leadership in order to serve the people and not to serve yourself.'[16] Some inevitably saw this as yet another moral stick wielded by Mbeki to beat his ethically challenged successor.

7

Legacy

Thabo Mbeki noted in January 2016 that, like former British prime minister Winston Churchill, he would try to write his own history so that it could be kind to him. Yet all that statesmen like Churchill and Mbeki can do is present their own subjective versions of history to set against other perspectives. They cannot impose their own views of the past on the public. Trying to do so is an exercise as futile as the fabled African rainmaker seeking to hold back the rain.

Mbeki was undoubtedly the most important political figure of his generation, both in South Africa and on the continent as a whole. He dedicated 52 years of his life to the African National Congress, of which more than half were spent in exile under often difficult circumstances. His commitment to the anti-apartheid struggle was total. After leading secret talks to reassure white captains of industry, intellectuals and eventually government officials and politicians that they could do business with the ANC, he went on to contribute significantly to building South Africa's new democratic constitutional order between 1990 and 1994. Thereafter, first as deputy president under Nelson Mandela and then as president in his own right for almost two terms, he led Africa's most industrialised state and largest economy at the time (it was overtaken by Nigeria in 2013). Mandela's own verdict on his successor, with whom he often had a complicated relationship, was characteristically generous: 'No president or prime minister in the history of this country can claim to have done more for the people and the country than has been achieved by President Thabo Mbeki.'[1]

His legacy will, inevitably, be a mixed one. On the positive side, he led efforts to extend basic services and facilities to millions of poor and previously disregarded black citizens, and, through a massive extension of social grants, helped lift many millions out of dire poverty and social misery. Domestically, the AIDS debacle in which his government became embroiled as a result of its delay in providing antiretroviral drugs to patients will be the greatest blot on his record. The effects of the controversial arms deal still reverberate nearly two decades later. His monarchical leadership style also led to accusations of an autocratic streak and an intolerance of dissent within his cabinet, party structures and parliament.

Yet Mbeki remained a constitutional monarch who stuck consistently to the rules of the democratic game. His autocratic leadership style was somewhat akin to that of Margaret Thatcher. Indeed, at a press conference on GEAR in June 1996, Mbeki said: 'Just call me a Thatcherite!'[2] Both leaders were dominant figures in their political parties who sought the socio-economic transformation of their societies through conservative, neo-liberal economic policies. Both were highly intelligent political players, dominating debates and brooking no dissent. Both in the end created too many enemies through their unbending belief in the righteousness of their own ideas. Both eventually suffered humiliating exits from power, 'recalled' from office by their own parties before the end of their tenure.

* * *

One guiding theme of Mbeki's time as president was his espousal of pan-Africanism. Despite criticisms of his so-called 'nativism' and 'Afrocentrism', Mbeki was absolutely correct to put race at the centre of debates on transformation in South Africa. Apartheid and its social divisions had, after all, determined privilege and poverty entirely on the basis of race. Ironically, though, while he championed an African Renaissance, the models that Mbeki often borrowed in order to provide the means for transformation of his country came from outside the continent: the British-inspired cabinet office, the

Malaysian-inspired BEE policy, and the white dominion-inspired OBE educational system. Perhaps this was because the great lesson that Mbeki – and other ANC leaders like Chris Hani – took away from their African exile was to avoid, at all costs, the autocratic governance and ruinous economic policies of their host countries once they had won South Africa's freedom.

It is in the area of foreign policy in Africa that Mbeki's historical achievements are likely to endure. Mbeki's pan-Africanism also embraced the African diaspora, as his activism and advocacy efforts in Haiti, Cuba, Brazil and the US demonstrated. He called for the end to 'global apartheid' and the democratisation of institutions of global governance such as the UN, the World Bank, the IMF and the WTO. Mbeki sought to work with influential countries like Brazil and India to increase the leverage of the global South in international politics, and he engaged the G-8 industrialised nations on behalf of Africa.

Mbeki was an active peacemaker, and his peacemaking ventures in the DRC, Zimbabwe and Burundi were noteworthy at the time and will remain among his most impressive successes. He devoted much effort, time, patience and intelligence to efforts that brought more stability to these countries and saved thousands of lives. The London-based *Economist* noted in October 2004 that Mbeki – instead of the Kenyan environmental activist Wangari Maathai – deserved the Nobel Peace Prize for that year, observing: 'Today the politician who has

161

arguably done the most to end the world's worst wars is South Africa's president, Thabo Mbeki, who was instrumental in pushing Congo and Burundi from utter mayhem to shaky peace,' before adding, 'Ah yes, you say, but he has controversial views on AIDS.'[3]

As regards his energetic peacemaking, one criticism that may linger is that Mbeki often supported the stronger party in disputes, thus eventually alienating the opposition in Côte d'Ivoire, Zimbabwe and South Sudan. But even the representative of one of Mbeki's arch-foes, the MDC finance minister, Tendai Biti, conceded: 'Zimbabwe and the GNU [Government of National Unity] remain one of Mbeki's greatest legacies.'[4]

Mbeki was instrumental in providing the vision for and helping establish a number of Africa-wide initiatives, organisations and institutions, including the African Union, NEPAD, the APRM, and the Pan-African Parliament (PAP), often on the basis of a strategic alliance with Nigeria's Olusegun Obasanjo. As it is often said about the UN, if these fragile institutions did not exist, they would still need to be created. The 15-member AU Peace and Security Council has played a significant role in efforts to manage African conflicts, but other institutions remain fledgling and the AU remains dependent on external donors to provide much of its resources. NEPAD, the APRM and the Pan-African Parliament are all based in South Africa. Both NEPAD and the APRM appear to be cash-strapped and increasingly irrelevant, and the attention they received during the Mbeki era has clearly disappeared. Only 17 of 35 countries had been reviewed by the APRM in 13 years, while the PAP remains a 'talking shop' with no substantive legislative powers.

* * *

The last of Mbeki's greatest legacies is the self-confidence and proud assertion of an African identity that he imparted particularly among South Africa's new black middle class. In South Africa, the continuing fascination with Mbeki's ideas and vision has been confirmed by two plays. *Mbeki and Other Nitemares*, written by Tsepo wa Mamatu and performed by the University of the Witwatersrand's drama school in 2010, revealed Mbeki's flaws and his tragic downfall, but also demonstrated the importance of his consistent insistence on excellence and African self-reliance for an aspiring black middle class.[5] In 2011 an experimental play, *Rhetorical* – written by Mpumelelo Paul Grootboom and Aubrey Sekhabi – drew on Mbeki's famous 'I am an African' and 'two nations' speeches, his 2008 resignation speech, and his 2006 Nelson Mandela memorial lecture. Since 2008, South Africa's second democratic president may not have been 'ruling from the grave', but his long shadow continues to loom over the country.

We end the book where we started, by returning to a comparison of Mbeki and Kwame Nkrumah as Africa's most prominent philosopher-kings of their ages.

Both leaders attempted to carry out a socio-economic revolution without genuine revolutionaries. Both lacked competent cadres and administrators in the numbers needed to ensure the success of their revolutions. But, while Nkrumah led a poor country that punched above its weight in global politics, Mbeki was the head of Africa's richest and most industrialised state, and there were thus greater expectations that his vision would succeed. However, South Africa's deep socio-economic inequalities and injustices remained stubbornly untransformed. Having worked so tenaciously to secure the political kingdom, both leaders discovered that all other things were not added unto it. Failure to deliver the economic kingdom in the end led to the political crucifixion of both prophets.

The Kenyan scholar Ali Mazrui famously argued in 1966 that Nkrumah was a great pan-African, but not a great Ghanaian. Five decades later, we ask: Will Mbeki come to be viewed in similar vein, as a great pan-African but not a great South African? When Nkrumah was ousted from power, an angry mob destroyed his statue, and streets named after him were changed. Within 26 years, Nkrumah's successors had so mismanaged the country that nostalgia for his memory returned. A new statue and memorial park were built in his honour in 1992 in an impressive act of national restitution. Will South Africans also come to view Mbeki more favourably with the passage of time?

Notes

INTRODUCTION

1 Mark Gevisser, *Thabo Mbeki: The Dream Deferred* (New York: Palgrave Macmillan, 2009) (US edition unless specified).

CHAPTER 1: AFRICA'S PHILOSOPHER-KINGS

1 This chapter builds on Adekeye Adebajo, 'Thabo Mbeki: A Nkrumahist Renaissance?' in *The Curse of Berlin: Africa after the Cold War* (Oxford: Oxford University Press, 2013), pp. 233–259.

2 Quoted in Mark Kingwell, 'Why Every Government Should Keep an Empty Seat for a Philosopher King,' *The Guardian* (London), 10 May 2012.

3 See, for example, Chris Alden and Maxi Schoeman, 'South Africa in the Company of Giants: The Search for Leadership in a Transforming Global Order', *International Affairs*, 89:1, 2013, pp. 111–129.

4 Ali A. Mazrui, 'The Monarchical Tendency in African Political Culture', in *Violence and Thought* (London: Longmans, 1969), p. 230.

5 See Ali A. Mazrui, 'Nkrumah: The Leninist Czar', in *On Heroes and Uhuru-Worship* (London: Longman, 1967), pp. 113–134.

6 Robert H. Jackson and Carl L. Rosberg, *Personal Rule in Black Africa* (Berkeley: University of California Press, 1982), p. 182.

7 Bankole Timothy, *Kwame Nkrumah: His Rise to Power* (London: Allen and Unwin, 1963), p. 172.

8   Thabo Mbeki, *Mahube: The Dawning of the Dawn* (Braamfontein: Skotaville, 2001), pp. 194–195.

9   Cited in Gevisser, *Thabo Mbeki*, p. xxxix. The paragraph is also based largely on this source.

CHAPTER 2: COMING OF AGE

1   This chapter draws heavily on Mark Gevisser, *Thabo Mbeki*, and Adrian Hadland and Jovial Rantao, *The Life and Times of Thabo Mbeki* (Rivonia: Zebra, 1999).

2   Quoted in Hadland and Rantao, *The Life and Times of Thabo Mbeki*, p. 14.

3   Quoted in Gevisser, *Thabo Mbeki*, p. 43.

4   Ibid., p. 208.

5   Ibid., p. 45.

6   Quoted in Hadland and Rantao, *The Life and Times of Thabo Mbeki*, p. 17.

7   Quoted in Gevisser, *Thabo Mbeki*, p. 75.

8   Thabo Mbeki, 'Oliver Tambo: "A Great Giant Who Strode the Globe like a Colossus"', in Z. Pallo Jordan (ed.), *Oliver Tambo Remembered* (Johannesburg: Pan Macmillan, 2007), p. xvi.

9   Cited in Chris McGreal, 'The Great Persuader', *The Guardian* (London), 29 May 1999.

10   Cited in Gevisser, *Thabo Mbeki*, p. 105.

11   Mbeki, 'Oliver Tambo', p. xix.

CHAPTER 3: THE PATH TO POWER

1   Gevisser, *Thabo Mbeki*, p. 111.

2   Ibid., p. 118.

3   Ibid., p. 139.

4   William M. Gumede, *Thabo Mbeki and the Battle for the Soul of the ANC* (Cape Town: Zebra, 2005), p. 33.

5   I am grateful for many of these insights to Hugh Macmillan, *Chris Hani* (Johannesburg: Jacana, 2014).

6   Confidential correspondence.

7   Gevisser, *Thabo Mbeki*, p. 121; Gumede, *Thabo Mbeki*, p. 40.

8   Gevisser, *Thabo Mbeki*, p. 122.

9   Ibid., p. 179.

10   I am grateful here to Gevisser, *Thabo Mbeki*, pp. 174–177.

11   Ibid., pp. 218, 131–132.

12   Hadland and Rantao, *The Life and Times of Thabo Mbeki*, p. 3;

Gevisser, *Thabo Mbeki*, pp. 141–149.

13 Gevisser, Thabo Mbeki, pp. 150–156.

14 Ibid., pp. 133–134.

15 Confidential correspondence.

16 Gevisser, *Thabo Mbeki* (Johannesburg: Jonathan Ball, 2007), pp. 377–388.

17 Ibid., pp. 374, 387.

18 Ibid., pp. 370–388.

19 Gevisser, *Thabo Mbeki* (US edn), p. 165.

20 Mbeki, 'Oliver Tambo', p. xvii.

21 Gumede, *Thabo Mbeki*, p. 37.

22 Ben Turok, *With My Head above the Parapet: An Insider Account of the ANC in Power* (Johannesburg: Jacana, 2014), p. 62.

23 Gevisser, *Thabo Mbeki*, pp. 166–167.

24 Confidential correspondence.

25 Gevisser, *Thabo Mbeki*, p. 170.

26 Quoted in ibid., p. 167.

27 Cited in ibid., p. 124.

28 Ibid., pp. 181–182.

29 Gumede, *Thabo Mbeki*, p. 38.

30 Confidential correspondence.

31 Gevisser, *Thabo Mbeki*, pp. 203–204.

32 Ibid., p. 182.

33 Ibid., p. 187.

34 Ibid., p. 195.

35 Ibid., p. 205. See also Macmillan, *Chris Hani*, p. 101.

36 Gevisser, *Thabo Mbeki*, p. 200.

37 Confidential correspondence.

38 Mbeki, 'Oliver Tambo', p. xviii.

39 Ibid.

40 Gevisser, *Thabo Mbeki*, pp. 205–207.

41 Ibid., p. 216.

42 Ibid., p. 217.

43 'Biographical Sketch of Thabo Mbeki', in Thabo Mbeki, *Africa: The Time Has Come* (Cape Town: Tafelberg and Mafube, 1998), p. xxi.

44 Gevisser, *Thabo Mbeki*, p. 226.

45 Confidential correspondence.

46 Confidential correspondence.

47 Quoted in Gumede, *Thabo Mbeki*, p. 64.

48 Ibid., p. 45.

CHAPTER 4: THE DOMESTIC PRESIDENT

1   Gevisser, *Thabo Mbeki*, p. 244.
2   Gumede, *Thabo Mbeki*, p. 32.
3   Quoted in Mbeki, 'Oliver Tambo', p. xx.
4   Transcript of interview with F.W. de Klerk by John Carlin (www.pbs.org/wgbh/pages/frontline/shows/mandela/interviews/deklerk.html), downloaded 6.1.2016.
5   Gevisser, *Thabo Mbeki*, p. 263.
6   Cited in ibid., p. 213.
7   Ibid., p. 264.
8   Gumede, *Thabo Mbeki*, p. 49.
9   Gevisser, *Thabo Mbeki*, p. 261.
10 Quoted in Gumede, *Thabo Mbeki*, p. 54.
11 Quoted in ibid., p. 33.
12 Confidential correspondence.
13 See Gumede, *Thabo Mbeki*.
14 Gevisser, *Thabo Mbeki*, p. xxiii.
15 Confidential correspondence.
16 Mahmood Mamdani, 'There Can Be No African Renaissance Without an Africa-Focused Intelligentsia', in M.W. Makgoba (ed.), *African Renaissance: The New Struggle* (Cape Town: Tafelberg, 1999), pp. 125–134.
17 Kader Asmal and Adrian Hadland, *Politics in My Blood: A Memoir* (Johannesburg: Jacana, 2011), p. 219.
18 Turok, *With My Head above the Parapet*, p. 48.
19 Asmal and Hadland, *Politics in My Blood*, p. 214.
20 Turok, *With My Head above the Parapet*, pp. 48–49.
21 Ibid., p. 53.
22 Thabo Mbeki, 'The Tragedy of History: When Caricature Displaces the Truth?', 11 January 2016, Thabo Mbeki African Leadership Institute Facebook page (www.facebook.com/thabombekiafricanleadershipinstitute).
23 Thabo Mbeki, 'When Your Position Can't Be Sustained, Create a Scarecrow: The Menace of Post-Apartheid South Africa', *Politicsweb*, 18 January 2016 (www.politicsweb.co.za).
24 Jeremy Cronin, 'Mbeki Still Doesn't Get It', *The Times* (South Africa), 20 January 2016 (www.timeslive.co.za).
25 Colin Bundy, *Short-Changed? South Africa since Apartheid* (Johannesburg: Jacana, 2014), p. 56.
26 *The Economist*, 'Thabo Mbeki: A Man of Two Faces', 20 January 2005.

27 For an example of this sort of writing, see Xolela Mangcu, *To the Brink: The State of Democracy in South Africa* (Scottsville: University of KwaZulu-Natal Press, 2008), pp. 131–152.

28 See, for example, Ronald Suresh Roberts, *Fit to Govern: The Native Intelligence of Thabo Mbeki* (Johannesburg: STE, 2007).

29 Megan Power and Jocelyn Maker, 'The R30 Million Bombshell That Points Fingers at Both Mbeki and His Former Deputy', *Sunday Times* (South Africa), 3 August 2008.

30 Turok, *With My Head above the Parapet*, p. 63.

31 Sarah Evans, 'Mbeki "Can't Recall" Deal Details', *Mail & Guardian*, 18 July 2014.

32 Cited in Brian Pottinger, *The Mbeki Legacy* (Cape Town: Zebra, 2008), p. 60.

33 Pixley Seme, 'The Regeneration of Africa', Columbia University, New York, 5 April 1906 (www.anc.org.za).

34 Quoted in Gevisser, *Thabo Mbeki*, p. 221.

35 Ibid., p. 264.

36 Mbeki, *Mahube*, pp. 4–5.

37 Mbeki, *Africa: The Time Has Come,* pp. 31–32.

38 Daryl Glaser, 'Mbeki and His Legacy: A Critical Introduction', in Daryl Glaser (ed.), *Mbeki and After* (Johannesburg: Wits University Press, 2010), pp. 3–40.

39 Steven Friedman, 'Being Ourselves as Others See Us: Racism, Technique and the Mbeki Administration', in Glaser (ed.), *Mbeki and After*, pp. 163–186.

40 Alan Hirsch, *Season of Hope: Economic Reform under Mandela and Mbeki* (Scottsville: University of KwaZulu-Natal Press, 2005), p. 4.

41 Friedman, 'Being Ourselves as Others See Us,' p. 183.

42 Cited in Mazrui, 'Nkrumah', pp. 122–123.

43 Gevisser, *Thabo Mbeki*, p. xxxi.

44 Mbeki, *Africa*, p. 76.

45 Hein Marais, *South Africa Pushed to the Limit: The Political Economy of Change* (Cape Town: University of Cape Town Press, 2011), p. 116.

46 Hirsch, *Season of Hope*, p. 2.

47 Marais, *South Africa Pushed to the Limit*, pp. 113–114.

48 Ibid., p. 117.

49 See Patrick Bond, *Talk Left, Walk Right: South Africa's Frustrated Global Reforms* (Scottsville: University of KwaZulu-Natal Press, 2004).

50 Gevisser, *Thabo Mbeki*, p. xxxiv.

51 Quoted in Vishwas Satgar, 'Thabo Mbeki and the South African Communist Party', in Sean Jacobs and Richard Calland (eds.), *Thabo Mbeki's World: The Politics and Ideology of the South African President* (Pietermaritzburg: University of Natal Press, 2002), p. 164.

52 Quoted in Marais, *South Africa Pushed to the Limit*, p. 112.

53 Bundy, *Short-Changed?*, p. 61.

54 Sampie Terreblanche, *Lost in Transformation: South Africa's Search for a New Future since 1986* (Johannesburg: KMM Review Publishing, 2012), p. 72.

55 Marais, *South Africa Pushed to the Limit*, p. 125.

56 Bundy, *Short-Changed?*, pp. 61–62.

57 Adam Habib, *South Africa's Suspended Revolution: Hopes and Prospects* (Johannesburg: Wits University Press, 2013), p. 80.

58 Marais, *South Africa Pushed to the Limit*, p. 126.

59 Bundy, *Short-Changed?*, p. 80.

60 Ibid., p. 62.

61 Terreblanche, *Lost in Transformation*, p. 80.

62 For a *mea culpa* by one of Mbeki's ministers, see Ronnie Kasrils, 'How the ANC's Faustian Pact Sold Out South Africa's Poorest', *The Guardian* (London), 24 June 2013.

63 Alan Hirsch, 'How Compromises and Mistakes Made in the Mandela Era Hobbled South Africa's Economy', *The Conversation*, 26 December 2015 (https://the conversation.com).

64 Quoted in Gevisser, *Thabo Mbeki*, p. 219.

65 Gumede, *Thabo Mbeki*, p. 224.

66 See, for example, Khehla Shubane, 'Black Economic Empowerment: Myths and Realities', in Adekeye Adebajo, Adebayo Adedeji and Chris Landsberg (eds.), *South Africa in Africa: The Post-Apartheid Era* (Scottsville: University of KwaZulu-Natal Press, 2007), pp. 63–77.

67 These are South African government figures cited in Mark Gevisser, 'Time of Reckoning', *BBC Focus on Africa Magazine*, 20:2, April–June 2009, p. 18.

68 Adebayo Adedeji, 'South Africa and Africa's Political Economy: Looking Inside from the Outside', in Adebajo, Adedeji and Landsberg (eds.), *South Africa in Africa*, pp. 40–62.

69 This paragraph draws from Marais, *South Africa Pushed to the Limit*, pp. 323–331.

70 Ibid., pp. 309–312.

71 See, for example, Angela Ndinga-Muvumba and Robyn Pharoah, *HIV/AIDS and Society in South Africa* (Scottsville: University of KwaZulu-Natal Press, 2008); and Nicoli Nattrass, *Mortal Combat: AIDS Denialism and the Struggle for Antiretrovirals in South Africa* (Scottsville: University of KwaZulu-Natal Press, 2007).

72 Mediaaids, '1997: The Virodene Controversy' (www.mediaaids, org).

73 Amy Green, 'From Critical Condition to Stable', *Mail & Guardian*, 11–16 April 2014, p. 6.

74 Mediaaids, 'Nkosazana Dlamini-Zuma' (www.mediaaids.org); and Kerry Cullinan, 'Frank Chikane's Whitewash of Mbeki Is an Historical Disgrace', Health-e, 5 November 2010 (www.health-e. org.za).

75 Patrick Bond, 'Globalization, Pharmaceutical Pricing, and South African Health Policy: Managing Confrontation with US Firms and Politicians', *International Journal of Health Services*, 29:4, 1999, p. 767.

76 Gevisser, *Thabo Mbeki*, p. 291.

77 Asmal and Hadland, *Politics in My Blood*, pp. 217–218.

78 See, for example, Roberts, *Fit to Govern*, pp. 180–241.

79 Gevisser, *Thabo Mbeki*, p. 245.

80 Mzukisi Qobo, 'ANC Must Rid Itself of Last Vestiges of Mbeki Era', *Business Day*, 11 May 2012.

81 Turok, *With My Head above the Parapet*, p. 74.

82 Cited in Richard Calland, *Anatomy of South Africa: Who Holds the Power?* (Cape Town: Zebra, 2006), p. 45.

83 Turok, *With My Head above the Parapet*, p. 94.

84 Andile Mngxitama, 'Zuma and Mbeki Are Two Sides of the Same Coin', *Sunday Independent*, 17 May 2009, p. 10.

85 Confidential correspondence.

86 Turok, *With My Head above the Parapet*, p. 75.

87 Achille Mbembe, 'South Africa's Second Coming: The Nongqawuse Syndrome', *Open Democracy News Analysis,* 14 June 2006, pp. 2–3.

88 Wole Soyinka, *The Lion and the Jewel* (London: Oxford University Press, 1963).

CHAPTER 5: THE FOREIGN POLICY PRESIDENT

1   This chapter builds on Adebajo, *The Curse of Berlin*.

2 Chris Alden and Garth Le Pere, 'South Africa's Post-Apartheid Foreign Policy: From Reconciliation to Revival?', Adelphi Paper 362, International Institute for Strategic Studies, London, 2003, p. 32.

3 Peter Vale and Sipho Maseko, 'Thabo Mbeki, South Africa, and the Idea of an African Renaissance', in Jacobs and Calland (eds.), *Thabo Mbeki's World*, p. 124.

4 See, for example, Annie Coombes, *History after Apartheid: Visual Culture and Public Memory in a Democratic South Africa* (Johannesburg: Wits University Press, 2004).

5 See J.S. Crush and David A. McDonald, introduction to 'Special Issue: Evaluating South African Immigration Policy after Apartheid', *Africa Today*, 48:1, 2001, pp. 1–13; Zimitri Erasmus, 'Race and Identity in the Nation', in John Daniel, Roger Southall, and Jessica Lutchman (eds.), *State of the Nation: South Africa 2004–2005* (Cape Town: Human Sciences Research Council Press, 2005), pp. 15–19; and Audie Klotz, 'Migration after Apartheid: Deracialising South African Foreign Policy', *Third World Quarterly*, 21:5, 2000, pp. 831–847.

6 James Barber, *Mandela's World: The International Dimension of South Africa's Political Revolution, 1990–99* (Cape Town: David Philip, 2004), p. 179.

7 John Daniel, Varusha Naidoo and Sanusha Naidu, '"The South Africans Have Arrived": Post-Apartheid Corporate Expansion into Africa', in John Daniel, Adam Habib and Roger Southall (eds.), *The State of the Nation: South Africa 2003–2004* (Cape Town: Human Sciences Research Council Press, 2003), pp. 376–377.

8 John Daniel, Jessica Lutchman and Sanusha Naidu, 'South Africa and Nigeria: Two Unequal Centres in a Periphery', in Daniel, Southall and Lutchman (eds.), *State of the Nation*.

9 This is summarised from the insightful article by John Daniel and Nompumelelo Bhengu, 'South Africa in Africa: Still a Formidable Player', in Roger Southall and Henning Melber (eds.), *A New Scramble for Africa? Imperialism, Investment, and Development* (Scottsville: University of KwaZulu-Natal Press, 2009), pp. 139–164.

10 Daniel, Naidoo and Naidu, '"The South Africans Have Arrived"', p. 368.

11 'A Strategic Appraisal of South Africa's Foreign Policy in Advancing the Agenda of Africa and the South', Draft discussion paper

compiled by the Policy, Research and Analysis Unit of the South African Department of Foreign Affairs for the Heads of Mission Conference, Cape Town, 17–21 February 2005.

12 James Barber and John Barratt, *South Africa's Foreign Policy* (Cambridge: Cambridge University Press, 1990), p. 124.

13 Mbeki, *Mahube*, pp. 179–183.

14 'Address by the President of South Africa, Thabo Mbeki, at the Celebrations of the Bicentenary of the Independence of Haiti: Port-au-Prince, 1 January 2004', South African History Online (www.sahistory.org.za).

15 Thabo Mbeki, 'Haiti after the Press Went Home,' *ANC Today*, 4:29, 23–29 July 2004 (www.anc.org.za).

16 The quotes in this paragraph are all from Achille Mbembe, '*Sacré Bleu!* Mbeki and Sarkozy?', *Mail & Guardian*, 24–30 August 2007, p. 24.

17 Ibid., p. 24.

18 Personal interview with George Nene, Tshwane, 22 July 2004.

19 Eghosa E. Osaghae, *Nigeria since Independence: Crippled Giant* (Bloomington: Indiana University Press, 1998), p. 309.

20 Quoted in Barber, *Mandela's World*, p. 110.

21 Adekeye Adebajo and Chris Landsberg, 'The Heirs of Nkrumah: Africa's New Interventionists', *Pugwash Occasional Paper*, 2:1, January 2000, pp. 65–90.

22 See Progress Report of the chair, Olusegun Obasanjo, to the third Ordinary Session of the Assembly of Heads of State and Government of the African Union, 6–8 July 2004, Addis Ababa, Ethiopia, NEPAD/HSGIC/07-2004/Doc 4, pp. 4–5.

23 Olusegun Obasanjo, 'Nigeria-South Africa: Bond across the Continent', in Ad'Obe Obe (ed.), *A New Dawn: A Collection of Speeches of President Olusegun Obasanjo*, vol. 2 (Ibadan: Spectrum Books, 2001), p. 137.

24 Department of Foreign Affairs of South Africa, *South Africa and Nigeria Bi-National Commission Communiqué*, Pretoria, 6 October 1999.

25 Agreed Minutes of the 6th Session of the Binational Commission between the Republic of South Africa and the Federal Republic of Nigeria held in Durban, South Africa, from 6 to 10 September 2004.

26 Confidential interview.

27 I am indebted here to Dianna Games, '"An Oil Giant Reforms": The Experience of South African Firms Doing Business in

Nigeria', Johannesburg: South African Institute of International Affairs, 2004, Business in Africa report no. 3.

28 See interview with Bangumzi Sifingo, in *Traders*, 13, February–May 2003, pp. 18–19.

29 See James Lamont, 'Mobile Phone Network Opens in Nigeria', *Financial Times*, 10 August 2001, p. 7; Games, 'An Oil Giant Reforms', p. 57; Daniel, Lutchman and Naidu, 'South Africa and Nigeria', pp. 559–560; Daniel and Bhengu, 'South Africa in Africa', p. 148.

30 Daniel and Bhengu, 'South Africa in Africa', pp. 149–150, 158.

31 Ibid., p. 149.

32 Confidential interviews.

33 Bond, *Talk Left, Walk Right*, pp. 112–113.

34 This information on Côte d'Ivoire has been drawn from the Fifth and Sixth Progress Report of the UN Secretary-General on the UN Operations in Côte d'Ivoire, S/2005/398, 17 June 2005; and S/2005/604, 26 September 2005 respectively.

35 Confidential interview.

36 Confidential interview.

37 I have relied here on the work of a Swedish scholar-diplomat intimately involved in Southern Africa during the anti-apartheid struggle. See Tor Sellström, *Sweden and National Liberation in Southern Africa, vol. 2: Solidarity and Assistance 1970–1994* (Uppsala: Nordiska Afrikainstitutet, 2002), pp. 679–692 and 794–810.

38 See Lloyd Sachikonye, 'South Africa's Quiet Diplomacy: The Case of Zimbabwe', in Daniel, Southall and Lutchman (eds.), *State of the Nation*, pp. 569–585.

39 'The Mbeki-Mugabe Papers: What Mbeki Told Mugabe', A Discussion Document, August 2001, *New Agenda*, 30, Second Quarter 2008, pp. 56–72.

40 Ibid., p. 72.

41 Vale and Maseko, 'Thabo Mbeki, South Africa', p. 132.

42 Patrick Bond, 'Zimbabwe, South Africa and the IMF', *South African Yearbook of International Affairs* (Johannesburg: South African Institute of International Affairs, 2006), p. 58.

43 Ibid., p. 59.

44 Christopher Landsberg, *The Quiet Diplomacy of Liberation: International Politics and South Africa's Transition* (Johannesburg: Jacana Media, 2005), p. 173.

45 See Dale McKinley, 'Commodifying Oppression: South African Foreign Policy Towards Zimbabwe under Mbeki', in Roger Southall (ed.), *South Africa's Role in Conflict Resolution and Peacemaking in Africa: Conference Proceedings* (Cape Town: Human Sciences Research Council, 2006), pp. 85–104; and Elizabeth Sidiropoulos and Tim Hughes, 'Between Democratic Governance and Sovereignty: The Challenge of South Africa's Africa Policy', in Elizabeth Sidiropoulos (ed.), *South Africa's Foreign Policy, 1994–2004: Apartheid Past, Renaissance Future* (Johannesburg: South African Institute of International Affairs, 2004), pp. 61–84.

46 Full transcript of former South African President Thabo Mbeki's Lecture at UNISA's Thabo Mbeki Leadership Institute. Delivered in Tshwane on 23 August 2013. *New Zimbabwe*, 30 August 2013 (www.newzimbabwe.com).

47 On Mbeki's mediation in the DRC, see Devon Curtis, 'South Africa: "Exporting Peace" to the Great Lakes Region?', in Adebajo, Adedeji and Landsberg (eds.), *South Africa in Africa*, pp. 253–273.

48 See, for example, Claude Kabemba, 'South Africa in the DRC: Renaissance or Neo-Imperialism?', in Sakhela Buhlungu, John Daniel, Roger Southall and Jessica Lutchman (eds.), *State of the Nation: South Africa 2007* (Cape Town: Human Sciences Research Council Press, 2007), pp. 533–551.

49 Cited in Judi Hudson, 'South Africa's Economic Expansion into Africa', in Adebajo, Adedeji, and Landsberg (eds.), *South Africa in Africa*, p. 138.

50 Report of the UN Secretary-General on Burundi, 4 December 2003, S/2003/1146, p. 10.

51 Musifiky Mwanasali, 'Emerging Security Architecture in Africa', Centre for Policy Studies, *Policy: Issues and Actors*, 7:4, February 2004, p. 14.

52 Ali A. Mazrui, *A Tale of Two Africas: Nigeria and South Africa as Contrasting Visions* (London: Adonis and Abbey, 2006), p. 206.

CHAPTER 6: THE POST-PRESIDENCY

1 For a perspective on the post-presidency, see Candice Moore, 'What Mbeki Did Next', *South African Journal of International Affairs*, 21:2, 2014, pp. 161–175.

2 *Zimbabwe Independent*, 'Too Late to Replace Mbeki – Analysts', 4 December 2008.

3   Confidential interviews.

4   Report of the UN Secretary-General on the AU–UN Hybrid Operation in Darfur, S/2010/382, 14 July 2010, p. 8.

5   Thabo Mbeki, 'What the World Got Wrong in Côte d'Ivoire', *Foreign Policy*, 29 April 2011.

6   Vijay Nambiar, 'Dear President Mbeki: The United Nations Helped Save the Ivory Coast', *Foreign Policy*, 17 August 2011.

7   Quoted in the UN Economic Commission for Africa, 'The High-Level Panel on Illicit Financial Flows Meets in Lusaka', 19 June 2003 (www.uneca.org).

8   'Track It! Stop It! Get It!' Report of the High-Level Panel on Illicit Financial Flows from Africa. Commissioned by the AU–ECA Conference of Ministers of Finance, Planning and Economic Development, 1 January 2015 (www.uneca.org).

9   The Thabo Mbeki Foundation website (www.thabombeki-foundation.org.za).

10 The Thabo Mbeki African Leadership Institute website (www. unisa.ac.za).

11 Thabo Mbeki, 'The African Union at 10: A Dream Deferred', *The Thinker*, September 2012.

12 Quoted in Patrick Bond, 'First Class Failure', *BBC Focus on Africa*, 21:4, October–December 2010, p. 26.

13 Quoted in David Smith, 'Mbeki Fears South Africa Is "Losing Sense of Direction"', *The Guardian* (London), 22 October 2012.

14 Vershani Pillay, 'Don't Betray Mandela's Legacy, Warns Mbeki', *Mail & Guardian*, 8 December 2013.

15 Quoted in Phakamisa Ndzamela, 'Cost of Our Freedom Must Not Be Squandered', *Business Day* (South Africa), 24 March 2014.

16 Quoted in Zandile Mbabela and Melitta Ngalonkulu, *The Herald* (South Africa), 2 November 2015.

CHAPTER 7: LEGACY

1   Quoted in André Grobler, 'AU Could've Wrapped Up Libya Conflict: Mbeki', *Mail & Guardian*, 20 August 2011.

2   Quoted in Patrick Bond, *Against Global Apartheid: South Africa Meets the World Bank, IMF and International Finance* (Cape Town: University of Cape Town Press, and London: Zed Books, 2013), p. ix.

3   *The Economist*, 'The Woman Who Planted Trees,' 14 October 2004.

4   Quoted in Moore, 'What Mbeki Did Next', p. 168.

5   I am grateful here to Mark Gevisser, 'From the Man Who Would Be King to the King Who Would Be Decapitated', *Mail & Guardian*, 8 November 2010.

Acknowledgements

Writing a book is a labour of love that always requires much collaboration. I would, firstly, like to thank the colleagues who gave me invaluable suggestions that helped to strengthen and shape this book, adding to both its substance and style: Pallo Jordan, Tor Sellström, Ben Turok, Devon Curtis, Gilbert Khadiagala and David Monyae. Friend, colleague and collaborator for over 25 years, Chris Landsberg has taught me more about Thabo Mbeki's foreign policy than any other scholar. Others who gave me invaluable insights in earlier work on Mbeki and Kwame Nkrumah were Kweku Ampiah, Ricardo Soares de Oliveira, Raufu Mustapha and Gavin Williams. Any errors in facts or judgement that remain in the book are, of course, my own responsibility.

I would, secondly, like to thank the institution I head, the Centre for Conflict Resolution (CCR) in Cape

Town, South Africa, for consistent support over the last 12 years. Many colleagues provided support that have helped shape my ideas, and the CCR librarian, Martha de Jager, tirelessly hunted down valuable sources for me at very short notice. I would also like to thank the funders of the Centre's Africa Programme, whose institutional support has helped it produce such important work on critical pan-African issues: the governments of Sweden, Norway, the Netherlands and Finland.

I would further like to thank Jacana Media. Russell Martin – who initiated the project – showed incredible patience throughout the process. As a Cambridge-educated historian, his remarkable editing skills were complemented by substantive insights which greatly enriched the book. I also thank Bridget Impey and other colleagues at Jacana who helped finalise the biography.

Finally, I would like to thank my family: 'Auntie', Tilewa, Kemi and Femi, whose support has always sustained all of my professional endeavours.

Index

183